Living Aboard Your
Recreational Vehicle

Living Aboard Your Recreational Vehicle

A Guide to the Fulltime Life on Wheels

by

Janet and Gordon Groene

ICS Books, Inc.
Merrillville, Indiana

LIVING ABOARD YOUR RECREATIONAL VEHICLE

Published by:
ICS Books, Inc.
One Tower Plaza
107 E. 89th Avenue
Merrillville, IN 46410

Library of Congress Cataloging-in-Publication Data

Groene, Gordon.
　　Living aboard your recreational vehicle.

　　Includes index.
　　1. Mobile home living.　2. Recreational vehicles.
I. Groene, Janet.　II. Title.
TX1105.G75　1986　　　643'.2　　　86-21359
ISBN 0-934802-31-9

Dedication

To M. & D. who kept the mail, and the faith. And to all the others whose homes stayed put but who always made room in their hearts and their lives for us.

Table of Contents

About the Authors

For the first 13 years of their marriage, the Groenes lived a comfortable, conventional lifestyle as Gordon pursued the aviation career he had trained towards since his teens. After eight years in Illinois, where Gordon flew for a division of Gulf & Western, the Groenes began thinking of a radical change in lifestyles.

They sold their home and most other possessions, bought a small sailboat, and cruised the Florida Keys and Bahamas for two years. They then added a motorhome which took them to the mountains for three to six months a year while they continued to cruise the tropics aboard their boat in winter.

Originally they'd planned to go back to what they now call "real life" when their savings were gone but soon they began turning Janet's writing background, and Gordons skill with a camera, into income. Their articles continue to appear in leading RV, yachting, travel, shelter, and general magazines. Their column on fulltime RV living appears monthly in Family Motor Coaching magazine.

After ten years fulltime on the go, with no home or furniture or telephone, they had a small home built. They continue to travel widely by boat, airline, the twin-engine airplane Gordon bought with monies realized from selling the boat, and in the original camper which they still own.

One of the questions they're asked most frequently is about children, with the implication that people with small children can't take up the wandering life. Although most RV fulltimers are either retirees, singles, or childless couples, it's very common for people who live aboard boats to bear and raise their families as they sail around the world. The subject of rearing and educating children on the go, for those who do want to enjoy RV fulltiming as a family, is covered in the Groene's *How to Live Aboard a Boat*, published by Hearst Marine Books. It can be ordered at any book store for $17.95 or ordered for $19.50 ppd. from Botebooks, Box 248, DeLeon Springs FL 32028.

Janet is also author of *Cooking on the Go,* a cookbook for sailors, campers, and other cooks who have very limited equipment and supplies. It too is published by Hearst, is available in book stores for $14.95, or can be ordered for $16.50 ppd. from the DeLeon Springs address.

An earlier edition of *Living Aboard Your Recreational Vehicle* was published in the late 1970's by David McKay Company. This volume is a complete rewrite and update, greatly expanded from the first book. Another Groene book, *The Galley Book* published by David McKay, is out of print.

PART ONE
Get Ready

Chapter 1
Song of the Open Road

We woke up to a thin, cold dawn and the pounding of a patrolman's fist on our camper door.

"Move along," he said, not unkindly. "I've let you sleep since 2:00 a.m. but it's six now and time you hit the road."

No, we weren't wino's sleeping on a park bench in Central Park, or tramps trying to snooze at the bus station. We'd stopped our RV at a highway rest plaza and had overslept the two-hour limit.

Our visit from the policeman was just another in a long series of reminders that, in shedding our old style of life and adopting a new role as fulltimer wanderers, we had lost a life-long mantle of respectability. Our taxes were paid up to date; we had no prison records; we were legally married and gainfully employed. Yet we now lived a life that baffled or amused many of the home-dwellers we met, and enraged a few.

Picture the free, roving life. Immediately you imagine a cozy, self-contained camper beside a rushing, trout-packed brook. You have no deadlines, no lawn to mow, no leaves to rake, no committees, no neighbors to endure year after year, no ties, no traps, no taxes. The fulltime RV life is all you hope for, and much, much, more. But it is also a break with treasured possessions, with status, with symbols, and with Our Place in Life.

The RV alone is a red flag in the face of the good burghers of many cities, where special laws has been passed against RV's for no other crime other than being RV's. In Fort Lauderdale, for example, a sign along the public beach prohibits the parking of campers there—even if your RV takes no more room than a car! Many other communities have laws against RV's staying within the city limits overnight, and some won't let you drive into town during the day either. We have, at various times, been hassled, threatened, vandalized, and humiliated.

It is not our aim to talk you out of following our mud flaps, but we do want to prick your dream balloon enough to bring you back to treetop level. In knowing there will be bitter with the better, you'll be better armed to make needed adjustments in yourself, in your dealings with society, and in your relationships with family and spouse.

For us, it all began back in Danville, Illinois, where Gordon was a corporate pilot. He liked the firm and the job, and he valued his friendships with his coworkers. We both liked Danville because it was large enough to have good shopping and a nice mix of people, yet small enough that I could get to the store on a bicycle and Gordon could get to the airport in only ten minutes. Still, we began to toy with the idea of early retirement just in case, as had happened with so many people we knew, time ran out before the magic age of 65.

Our own wandering life began in a sailboat, but that's another story told in our book *How to Live Aboard a Boat*, published by Hearst Marine Books. After cruising the Florida Keys and Bahamas for a couple of years, we bought a mini-motorhome to take north to the cool mountains, and to visit our families, in summer. For ten years we were rootless, routeless wanderers, spending our summers in the RV and our winters in the Bahamas aboard the boat.

The same problems were with us ashore and afloat. We had only a forwarding address, no telephone, no business address, never a local bank, and seldom a local citizen to vouch for us. We were joyously free, deliciously anonymous.

After ten years on the go we were ready for new challenges so we bought land near Daytona Beach, had a small house built where we have a spacious office for our writing, sold the boat, bought an airplane, and became part-time RV travelers again. If the fulltime RV life does nothing else, it lets you "live" in hundreds of communities while you decide where you want to spend the years after you settle down again. We would never have had the time to choose our new community so carefully, if we hadn't been living in the RV.

What Kind of Fulltiming is for You?

The whole, broad camping culture divides into several sub-categories, and much of your happiness and success in fulltiming depends on finding just the right niche for yourself. For many people, the camping itself is the whole nine yards. There are camping clubs, meetings, rallies, and group caravans. These clubs are especially popular with retirees because they provide both camaraderie and practical help. A half dozen couples fulltime as part of TL Enterprises, attending Good Sam rallies and participating almost year-round in group efforts.

Some RV owners are part-timers, many of them young families who camp as a low-cost way of vacationing. We know one such family, the parents both teachers, who live in a house during the school year and RV fulltime all summer.

Other people who fulltime part of the year are retirees, or people who professions require them to work only in certain seasons. Many of these people keep their homes, and live in them when they are not on the road. Others live fulltime in RV's but have only two "homes"—one campground in the North, and another in the Sunbelt.

For many people, the RV life is everything. For others, it serves only as a portable home base while they pursue some other way of life: sports car racing, surfing, lecturing, surveying, painting, working in carnivals or rodeos, or following a career in construction. For ourselves, the motorhome made a comfortable, mobile home and office while we established ourselves as a travel writer-photographer team.

For us and others like us, the RV living is incidental, and we have little in common with those for whom the RV itself is a total lifestyle. We enjoy the company of other campers when we encounter them, but we have never attended an RV rally. Our travel and social lives center around writing and photography, just as many other full-timers' lives center around aircraft meets, bass tournaments, or art shows.

Exploding Some Myths

Myth: By living in an RV, you can avoid taxes and live on almost nothing. Reality: Fuel, oil, tires and other supplies cost real money. Campground fees are flying higher ($25 a night is not uncommon), and you'll continue to pay taxes—sales, vehicle, income, and property taxes (which are included in campground rental fees).

Myth: Wanderers have no responsibilities, no cares, no problems. Reality: Not only do you have all the old problems of cooking, housekeeping, staying on a diet, doing the Christmas shopping, making ends meet—but a million new ones such as finding acceptable campsites, staying alive on the highway, and getting by with less living space than a German shepherd is allotted at the county pound. You're now living in a very complex lash-up of living quarters, plumbing, wiring, sewage, engine, and chassis — all of which you have to maintain yourself.

Myth: It's like a second honeymoon, just the two of you on an endless highway of travel delights. Reality: After a week in close quarters, your relationship may look less like a honeymoon and more like the Texas Chainsaw Massacre.

Myth: No more winter. Reality: It is possible to follow the seasons, but crowds and high prices go with you. It's even worse if you decide to winter over in a cold climate because RV's aren't insulated like homes. Fuel costs will be high, and comforts elusive.

Myth: Wide-open spaces. Reality: Only in RV ads is one camper given exclusive rights to the entire Grand Canyon. In most campgrounds you'll be closer to your neighbor than you ever were back in New Jersey.

Myth: We'll leave all our problems behind. Reality: Troubles are an unseen trailer that follow all of us everywhere. Look at the RV life as a way of running to new adventures and experiences, not as an escape from alcohol, marital problems, or debts.

Part of our success in coping with fulltime travel is that we not only expected most of the problems but that we welcomed them as new challenges. In exchange for the hardships of fulltime travel, we have formed priceless friendships with folks in many states and several foreign countries, and we have been freed from former careers to develop a new one as a freelance writer-photographer team.

To change lifestyles, no matter how flexible we consider ourselves, is a tough assignment. The rest of this book is our effort to help you through the roadblocks, breakdowns, detours, and potholes ahead.

Chapter 2
How to Retire Before 40

The key question now is: how can you begin now to prepare for an early retirement?

1. *Get your priorities straight.* Sit down with your family and decide what really matters to you. If fulltime travel is really your goal, begin preparations today. Go beyond romantic reveries of far-away places, and aimless pipedreams. Rehearse retirement by making a motorcoach trip of at least 3 weeks (longer if you can get off work). During this time you'll encounter some hints of the fulltimer's life: rainy days when you're shut in, mechanical problems, finding campgrounds, using coin laundries, finding your way around strange cities, trying to cash a check or use credit cards in strange cities, getting mail, walking the dog, planning your own hours with no job and no boss, and living day after day with very limited space. It will also give you an idea of what expenses you'll encounter: camp fees, mileage, restaurants and groceries, perhaps a breakdown or repair.

This isn't the entire story. You'll still have a home to retreat to, an address, and identity, storage at home for your off-season clothes, and many other perks which the fulltimer doesn't have. But it's a preview that's far cheaper and less wearing than selling the house and quitting your job *before* you find out you can't stand the uncertainty of living on the go or the discomfort of living in a home that is only 8' wide. And, believe it or not, many people find it boring not to have a job and a schedule.

2. *Get out of debt.* This is easier said than done, but start by mopping up all the little obligations: credit cards, time payments, all the petty loans. Saving up for a big purchase is an old American custom that has been entirely lost today, so we end up on a treadmill of monthly payments which the British call the never-never. When you take on a debt, you're spending money you haven't yet earned. So your earnings can't go into savings for your future, because they're already assigned to color TV, a car which will be worn out before it's paid for, a VCR, cemetary lots, clothes, and other things you may not even want when you're fulltiming.

3. *Get control of your health.* How many people do you know whose dreams of early, active retirement were shattered by ill health? Today's biggest health problems are overweight, alcoholism, highway accidents, and tobacco, all of them cripplers which you can choose—right now—to eliminate from your life. Obesity, alcoholism and tobacco dependence can be treated; your chances of being seriously injured on the road will be reduced dramatically if you wear a seatbelt.

4. *Live for tomorrow without sacrificing today.* From the moment we decided we wanted to retire early, we began buying everything with resale in mind. We continued to enjoy a spacious home, good cars, occasional travel, and the good life in general, weighing every purchase not just for its present value but for its resale potential. We could have afforded a better home in a swankier neighborhood, but we chose instead a big, old, 5-bedroom house near a couple of good schools, knowing it would sell readily to a big family. Our

car was an expensive Porsche, but Gordon groomed it meticulously, always washing off the salt after winter driving. It was kept garaged, and we always parked at the far end of parking lots so it wouldn't get nicked and scraped. Our furniture was good quality, in a traditional style that doesn't become outdated, and in solid woods that could be refinished if they were damaged. Many of the pieces were antiques which we refinished ourselves, and sold at a profit. Appliances were brand names. We lived well but kept things in the best condition possible. The money we got from selling everything helped fund our early retirement. We had some savings and investments, but we know one couple who completely bank-rolled a two-year odyssey with their two girls with the proceeds of a home they had renovated and antiques they had refinished.

5. *Get your financial picture in order.* We're no experts in investments but, for peace of mind on the road, it's important to have today's, and tomorrow's, obligations figured out. One couple established trust funds to pay their children's college tuition before they took off. Another, older couple encouraged an elderly parent to sell a too-large house, and move into a life-care retirement home so she'd have care if she became ill and the couple couldn't be reached on the road. Depending on your age and situation, you may want an annuity, income stocks, an IRA, rental properties, or other security, not just for yourselves but for dependent children, siblings or parents.

Some fulltimers have a modest kitty, and work as they go to replenish it. Our decision was to take our savings and roam until they were gone, then start fresh. After all, we'd only be in our 40's and we gambled that our robust health would hold. Decide for yourselves at what point you need to go back to work. Some people get edgy when their savings fall below $100,000; others feel rich with $1 in their pockets.

6. *Don't burn your bridges.* We all muse sometimes about telling the boss to "take this job and shove it", but you may someday want to go back to the same company, the same

city, the same social group. Even if you don't go back, you may someday need a job recommendation or a character reference from former associates.

7. *Take it slow; think it through.* The fun part is buying the coach, but don't buy your fulltimer RV too early if you can't also enjoy it, pay for it, and maintain it. On the other hand, if you sell your home and workshop too early, you won't have the tools to do the inevitable customizing every fulltimer coach needs. If you quit your job too soon you may end up without a salary while you're keeping up mortgage payments and trying to sell the house. If you sell the house too soon you may make too quick a decision on a coach. Lots of things have to dovetail, so don't act hastily.

8. *Sit down with pencil and paper and project your fulltiming costs.* Many fulltiming forays falter when money proves to be too big a problem, so re-read the chapter on costs and do some pencil work.

9. *Don't let possessions run your life.* Cautious people who have told us they'd love to go fulltiming, but couldn't part with their library, or Hummel collection, or billiard table. Your fulltiming life can't get off the ground until you can part with all the pounds of impedimenta that clutter your home, and it will be difficult to stay on the road if you fill the coach with souvenirs and brickabrack.

10. *Develop interests and hobbies.* Much has been written about the trauma of retirement, when suddenly you're an ex-somebody. As much as you may yearn for fulltiming, it may be more of a shock than you realize to give up your profession, furniture and home all at once. It helps to be involved with more than just travel because there are days when you don't feel like driving, or the weather is bad, or your fuel budget is strained, or you're hold up for repairs.

There are many compact and rewarding hobbies you can continue in your coach: ham radio, crewel embroidery, painting, macrame, learning to use a computer, and so on. You might also take up a hobby based on your travels: gravestone rubbings, sketching monuments, photographing state capitols, etc. Such hobbies give you purpose and identity, something to do on rainy days, and social focus when you're in new areas.

11. *Network.* Join the Good Sam Club, Family Motor Coaching Association, retiree groups, professional organizations, camping and travel clubs, hobby groups. The list is endless. If you're handicapped, single, widowed, or suffering from a special disease or disability, there are also organizations for you. By networking you can keep current on the job market in your field, get group discounts and insurance, learn about important gatherings having to do with your profession or hobby. Such groups can lobby to protect your interests, provide special information you need, and give you many other types of physical, financial, and emotional support. Because it may be difficult to connect or qualify after you're on the road, join before you take off.

12. *Keep as many options open as possible.* If you can get a leave of absence rather than quitting your job, do so. Make your first trip a modest one so you aren't in Alaska or Baja if you decide fulltiming isn't for you. Set milestones for yourself so you can keep reevaluating. For instance, you might agree to re-think the lifestyle after 2 years, or after you reach a certain age, or when your savings get down to $X. It isn't necessary to sign a blood oath that you'll roam the highways forever. If you have set times for re-commitment, you'll feel less locked in. Keep learning, searching, growing. Keep reassessing your goals, your chances, your pleasures, your present, your future. Go. Do. Enjoy.

Readers who want more information on this topic can benefit from reading *Managing Your Escape* by Katy Burke. It's published by Seven Seas Press which is distributed by Simon and Schuster.

Chapter 3
The Handicapped Fulltimer

Nelson W., age 70, is a stroke victim with limited use of his left side. Wanda S., 46, has multiple sclerosis and spends most of her time in a wheelchair. Harvey T., 38, was wounded during the Vietnam War, and will never regain the use of his legs. All are on disability yet all have North America at their doorsteps. Like hundreds of other handicapped people, they all turned injury and illness into victory by moving full-time into specially-equipped RV's.

If you think your dream of fulltiming has been shattered because of a handicap, think again. Motorcoach living can be a joy to anyone, but to the disabled it can provide more comfort, reward and mobility than any other way of life.

A good place to begin is by writing the Recreational Vehicle Industry Association, P.O. Box 2999, Reston Chantilly VA 22090. Enclose a stamped, self-addressed envelope and ask for their list of RV firms which manufacture coaches or accessories for the handicapped traveler. Most of the names are familiar, such as Beach-Craft, Barth, Airstream, and

11

Foretravel. These and other motorcoach builders offer custom designs, and have worked before to accommodate the handicapped. Others manufacture wheelchair lifts, ramps, hand controls, and other special equipment.

Foretravel, for example, sent me a floor plan for one of their most popular wheelchair-accessible coaches. It's 35′ long, and is built on a Roadmaster chassis with a Chevrolet 454 or Detroit Diesel 8.2 engine. Under the walnut paneling on the walls there are additional supports so hand pulls, handles and brackets can be added. There are special light switches, space under the sinks so the wheelchair can be pulled up to them, a wide door and a lift so a person in a wheelchair can enter, and lots of floor space inside for a wheelchair, "There is virtually no limit to the many different floorplans we have available for the handicapped," says marketing director Robert McGrath.

For $3.50 you can get "Camping in the National Park System" from the Superintendent of Documents, U.S. Government Printing Office, Washington D.C. 20402. It lists campgrounds which are accessible to the handicapped, and outlines facilities such as paths and fishing piers that accommodate wheelchairs. Most states and some cities also publish travel guides for the handicapped, usually available free. At the beginning of each state listing in Woodall's Camping Directory (distributed by Simon and Schuster and available in book stores) are listed addresses where you can get tourism information from that state plus some of its cities and regions. Send a postcard to areas you plan to visit, asking for any travel guides they have for the disabled.

Other helpful books include *Access to the World*, published by Chatham Square Press, *The Wheelchair Traveler* by Douglass R. Annand, Ball Hill Rd., Milford NH 0305, and *Travel Ability*, published by Macmillan. Book stores can order these books for you, and a good book shop clerk may be able to suggest others.

Write the Travel Information Center, Moss Rehabilitation Hospital, 12th at Tabor, Philadelphia PA 19141 and the Easter Seal Society, Travel Information, 2023 W. Ogden, Chicago IL 60612. Both are sources of more help. If you need help in learning how to drive with a handicap, contact the Independent Living Hospital Driver Education Center, 615 N. Michigan St., South Bend IN 46601.

Depending on your disability you can also get information, and sometimes even equipment or financial aid, from an organization devoted to your particular disease or handicap. Veterans, especially with service-connected disabilities, have many helps and benefits available from the government.

Other organizations include the National Paraplegia Foundation, 333 N. Michigan Ave., Chicago IL 60601; National Amputation Foundation, 12-45 150th St., Whitestone NY 11357; International Society for Prosthetics and Orthotics, 1440 N. St. NW, Washington D.C. 20005; and the Disabled Officers Association, 1612 K St. NW, Suite 408, Washington D.C. 20006. There are dozens more. A good reference librarian can help you find the addresses of organizations that fit your special needs. You may have to write to several. Some such organizations specialize in serving victims; others only raise funds for research, prevention or education.

A free catalogue that specializes in clothing, tools, aids and gadgets for all types of handicaps and unusual needs is Comfortably Yours, 52 W. Hunter Ave., Maywood NJ 07607. They offer everything from cane that turns into a little stool to left-handed potato peelers and a table that fits into a wheelchair. I also recommend a subscription to *Accent on Living*, Box 700, Bloomington, IL 61701. It's an upbeat, encouraging view of the world of the disabled, filled with how-to articles and ads for ingenious equipment specific to the needs of the handicapped.

Bad luck can overtake any of us, any time. Thanks to the RV, however, we can leave hard luck behind and drive away—more free in some ways than healthy people who are chained to a house without wheels.

Chapter 4
What's Available in RVs

Dozens of manufacturers and hundreds of RV retailers compete for the dollars we spend on our live-aboard RVs. By visiting dealers in your hometown, you can step aboard many models and get the "feel" of construction, size, livability, and special features. Then, by writing to manufacturers, you can get a larger picture of what's available in RVs around the country and ask the name of your nearest dealers.

Other excellent sources of information are the more than a score of monthly publications for campers and RV owners. There are also nearly a dozen buyer and user guides on the market that are updated yearly with new model and price information. You may want to subscribe to some of these, or get copies at your library. Most of them carry advertising on the new product lines and have well-written articles on special features, maintenance and the RV lifestyle by technical experts or RV owners. They will help you learn what to look for in the market place.

There's even an organization especially for people who "live aboard" their RVs full time; obviously it would be a good resource for information. You can write the Fulltimer's Chapter, c/o FMCA, 8291 Clough Pike, Cincinnati OH 45244.

The interior of your live-aboard RV can be as simple or as luxurious as you want it to be; there's a floor plan to suit every need. Interiors are beautiful; birch paneling with upholstering in rich tones of plum, blue, or brown velour provide a contemporary look. If you prefer, there are the tweedy mixes for a sportier, rugged look.

Window treatments may include woven or solid blinds with simple curtains or valances to blend with the carpeting and upholstery for a total look—just like the home you left behind.

Just like back home, too, you will find an efficient kitchen. Every inch of space counts in providing convenience. There are stainless steel sinks, two-door refrigerators, two or four-burner ranges with an oven (even microwave ovens), pantry shelves and cupboards, as well as standing closets and overhead storage areas.

The manufacturers have also considered energy conservation in the construction of the units to make them energy and economically efficient. RVs are lighter in the 80s, but still rugged and sturdy enough for comfortable living. More efficient insulation, greater uses of aluminum or honeycomb materials, lighter construction of furnaces, generators, radial tires, diesel or LP-gas as fuel are modifications that may be found to help assure that your RV home will be a conservation home.

Another good way to get the "feel" of an RV—and RV living—is to rent one for a trip. This will help you decide on features that you want to look for in the unit that you buy.

If you have special needs that must be built in to a unit (such as features that are necessary for the physically handicapped), these can be accommodated, too. Your dealer will know which manufacturers can build to your specifications.

Above all, you want to consider SAFETY when you do your RV shopping. While the *safe operation* of the RV is the ultimate responsiblity of you, the owner, there is a basic "safety philosophy" built into the unit by the manufacturer who belongs to the Recreation Vehicle Industry Association (RVIA). That means the buyer, YOU, are in luck.

STANDARDS PROTECT THE BUYER

The By-Laws of RVIA require that members of the organization must certify that each RV they build complies with the American National Standard for Recreation Vehicles, the only nationally recognized consensus standard for these vehicles. It has more than 500 specifications that fill a 105-page book and cover the electrical, plumbing and heating systems of the RV. It was established by an American National Standards Committee under the aegis of the American National Standards Institute (ANSI).

Two other RVIA membership requirements affect the day-in, day-out operation of the manufacturer—and the ultimate product that rolls out his factory door. He must agree to frequent, unannounced visits by RVIA's professional staff of inspectors, who monitor the manufacturing process to determine the level of compliance to the standard. The manufacturer who does not maintain satisfactory compliance faces expulsion from RVIA.

In addition, the RVIA member manufacturer must affix a seal on each completed vehicle (near the door) by which he certifies that the unit complies to the American National Standard for Recreational Vehicles and the National Electrical Code.

Some 13 states require that all RVs sold within their borders be built to the standard—but more than that, some 90% of all RVs sold within the USA are built by members of RVIA. Since they must build to the standard to maintain their membership, you would do well to ask your retailer to show you the RVs that carry the RVIA seal. By the same token, when repairs or replacement parts are necessary after purchase

RVIA Seal

of the unit, you should *demand* that the retailer or the servicing firm follow ANSI specifications.

The RV standard has four main sections that cover Fire and Life Safety features, and the Plumbing, Electrical, and LP-Gas Systems of the RV.

FIRE AND LIFE SAFETY

Minimum flamespread ratings are specified for interior walls and ceilings.

Fire extinguishers are required if the vehicles are e-quipped with fuel-burning appliances or an internal combustion engine.

A minimum of two egress means is required . . . and alternative exits must be labeled.

Generator units which are driven by internal combustion engines must be installed in a vapor-tight compartment to the interior of the vehicle.

PLUMBING SYSTEMS

Approval of all fixtures, fittings, materials and equipment by a testing agency such as the National Sanitation Foundation or the International Association of Plumbing and Mechanical Officials is required. After certification all components must display the insignia of the approving agency.

Water supply lines must be sized according to the number of fixtures to assure an adequate flow rate. Sanitizing instruction for periodic cleansing of the water system must be furnished with each vehicle, and the system must be capable of having drainage by gravity with a valve, drain plug or cap.

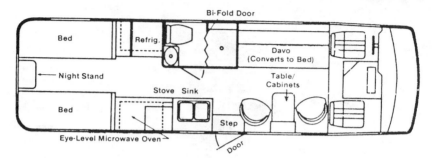

Typical Floor Plan—Motor Home

The drainage system requirements are intended primarily to eliminate the possibility of the entrance of sewer gas into the interior atmosphere, and water seal traps are specified in the drain line of each plumbing fixture except for approved toilets that have a mechanical seal.

Drain outlets must be at specified locations and venting of each drain line is required to prevent the build-up of back pressure or vacuums which could overcome the water seal in trap or siphon off the water and defeat the purpose of the trap. Waste holding tanks must be vented to dissipate gas and odors and to enable complete, unimpeded discharge at sanitation stations.

Testing of each vehicle's water supply and drainage systems must be performed by the RV manufacturer to determine that it is leak-free before leaving the factory.

ELECTRICAL SYSTEMS

While many of the requirements of the RV standard are based on the National Electrical Code which governs electrical safety principles in the home, there are some differences between home and RV application

All electrical fixtures, appliances, equipment and materials used in or connected to the 115-volt electrical systems carry the approval and listing of a nationally recognized testing agency such as Underwriters' Laboratory.

The exterior power supply cord must be factory installed or supplied to insure that it has sufficient current carrying capacity to handle the vehicle's system.

The distribution panelboard must provide the equipment necessary to safely connect an outside source of power to the various branch circuits within the system. It must provide protection to circuits, appliances and equipment by using devices like fuses or circuit breakers to cut off power when current exceeds the circuit's capacity.

Proper electrical grounding is essential as a final safeguard against electrical shock. Specific provisions of the standard are designed to achieve proper grounding to avoid a hazardous electrical shock. The distribution panelboard must provide for interconnecting an electrical grounding path from the external source of electricity to all metallic parts of the vehicle that may become energized and all exposed metallic parts of the electrical system.

Receptacle outlets are prohibited in bathtub or shower areas, but they are required in all other interior locations in sufficient quantity to handle normal needs without the use of extention cords or outlet multipliers.

Branch circuit specifications depend on the total number of lighting and receptacle outlets installed and on the total rating of the fixed appliances.

High voltage tests must be performed by the RV manufacturer on the completed electrical system to determine that it is adequately insulated and to avoid potential short circuits.

LP-GAS SYSTEMS

The LP-Gas systems are intended to minimize any hazard of fire or explosion which may occur as a consequence of a leak of LP-Gas in any part of the system and to assure proper appliance venting for prevention of asphyxiation.

The LP-Gas container supplied by the RV manufacturer must conform to the standards of the American Society of Mechanical Engineers (ASME) or the U.S. Department of Transportation (DOT). Both require that containers be tested to withstand excessive pressure and they must also be e-quipped with a safety-relief valve designed to discharge gas whenever internal pressure becomes excessive because of extreme temperature.

Gas piping must be large enough to assure that gas appliances receive sufficient gas to function properly.

Gas tubing made of copper, steel or brass cannot be installed in areas where it could be punctured by fasteners such as nails or screws unless protected by a metal conduit. Nor can a pipe or tubing joint be installed in a concealed construction space where it would be inaccessible for leakage testing or repair.

Appliances must be certified by a nationally recognized testing laboratory such as the American Gas Association (AGA) or Underwriters' Laboratories (UL).

Clearances must be sufficient in heat-producing appliance to prevent ignition of adjacent combustible surfaces.

Leakage testing must be performed by the RV manufacturer on the complete piping system before and after appliances are connected.

Sealed combustion must be provided for all LP-gas appliances except for gas ranges and gas lights to provide a complete separation of the combustion chamber from the atmosphere of the vehicle. An LP-gas heater, for instance, must use only air outside the RV for combustion and its exhaust gases must be vented to the outside.

More Information Available

As you can well realize, the RV standard is designed to protect you so that your RV will give you years of safe, comfortable happy wandering. If you should like a list of the publications for RV owners, simply send a stamped, self-addressed, *long* envelope to the Recreation Vehicle Industry Association, P.O. Box 2999, Dept. LARV, Reston, VA 22090. If you want a list of manufacturers who build units that will accommodate wheelchairs or other features for the handicapped, follow the same directions and send your long, self-addressed envelope to the same address, but make it for Dept. HWC.

For visual details on the RV standards and how the units

are built to conform, we suggest you ask your retailer to show you RVs that are built by members of the Recreation Vehicle Industry Association. A list of these follows, plus coded information which indicates the types of units that each produces.

Manufacturers' Product Codes

TT — Travel Trailers	MA — Motor Homes Type A
PT — Park Trailer	MB — Motor Homes Type B
FW — Fifth Wheel	MC — Motor Home Type C
FC — Folding Camping Trailer	VC — Multi-Use Van Conversions
TC — Truck Computer	PU — Pick Up Covers

A.B.E. Corporation, R.R. 3 Box 536, Syracuse, IN 46567,   VC
ABI Leisure, P.O.B. 308, 181 S. Service Rd., Grimbsy, Ontario, CANADA L3M 4G5,   TT
Action Interiors, Inc., 16551 Burke Lane, Huntington Beach, CA 92647, VC
Advanced Creations, Inc., 30415 Ecorse Road, Romulus, MI 48174   VC
Alfa Leisure, Inc., 5163 "G" Street, Chino, CA 91710,   FW, PT, TT
Amercon, Universal Auto Marketing, 1950 Jimmie Daniel Road, Bogart, GA 30622,   VC
American Custom Vans, Div. MWS Corp., 1800 Sherwood Forest, Bld. E, Houston, TX 77043,   VC
American Vans, Inc., Route 3, Box 380 Danielsville, GA 30633,   VC
Anaheim Vans, 2305 Bennington, Houston, TX 77093,   VC
Andy's Manufacturing, 7900 North Highway 52, Minneapolis, MN 55445,
                                                                   FC
Apex, Ivory Coach, 5600 S. Beltline Road, P.O. Box 53519 Mesquite, TX 75181,   VC
B & B Homes, Teton International, P.O. Box 2349, Mills, WY 82644,
                                                             FW, PT, TT
Barth, Inc., P.O.B. 768, State Road 15, S., Milford, IN 46542,   MA
Beachcomber of Sacramento, 3300 W. Capitol Avenue, W. Sacramento, CA 95691,   VC
Beaver Coaches, Inc., 20545 Murray Rd., Bend, OR 97701,   MA
Becker Auto Sales, 1457 N. Arizona Ave., Chandler, AZ 85224,   VC
Benicia Import Auto Services, 1 Oak Rd., Benicia, CA 94510   VC
Big A Van Conversions, 8650 Compton Blvd., Paramount, CA 90723, VC
Bigfoot Industries Ltd., R.R. #3, C-65 Pallisades, Armstrong, British Columbia CANADA VOE 1B0,   FW, TC, TT
Bivoauc Industries, P.O.B. 279, Vandalia, MI 49095,   VC
Blue Bird Wanderlodge, P.O.B. 1259, One Wanderlodge Way, Ft. Valley GA 31030,   MA
Bonair Leisure Industries Ltd., 755 Pope Street, P.O. Box 340, Cookshire, Quebec JOB 1MO,   FC

Cabriolet, U.S. 131 South 67351, Constantine, MI 49042,   VC
California Comfort Vans, 8150 Electric Ave., Stanton, CA 90803,   VC
Carriage, Inc., #5 Industrial Park, Millersburg, IN 46543,   FW, TT
Casa Villa Inc., 33 Industrial Park, P.O. Box 581, Goshen IN 46526,PT, TT
Centurion - Lehman, Inc., P.O. Box 715, U.S. 131 South, White Pigeon,
MI 49099,   VC
Century Motor Coach, Inc., 53387 Ada Drive, Elkhart, IN 46514,   VC
Celebrity Coach, Inc., 700 E. Main St., Larksville, PA 18651,   MB, VC
Champion Home Builders Co., 5573 North St., Dryden, MI 48428,   MA,
                                                                        MB, MC, VC
Chariot Vans, 28582 Jamie St., Sachs Industrial Pk, Elkhart, IN 46514-
9224,   VC
Chateau Recreational Vehicles, P.O.B. 9, 48-52 Mill St., Christiana, PA
17509,   FW, TT
Chesapeake Classics, P.O. Box 239, 700 Race St., Cambridge MD 21613,
                                                                                VC
Choo Choo Customs, 7751 Lee Highway, Chattanooga, TN 37412,   VC
Chupp & Sons Conversions, Inc., 57884 County Rd 3, Elkhart, IN 46517VC
Classic Conversions, 17511 Susana Rd., Rancho Dominguez, CA 90221VC
Classy Chassis Vans, Inc., 100 Axe Ave., Valparaiso, IN 46383,   VC
Coachmen Industries, Inc., 601 East Beardsley Ave., P.O. Box 3300, Elkhart,
In 46515,   FC, FW, MA, MB, MC, PT, TC
The Coleman Company, RD #2, P.O. Box 111, Somerset, PA 15501
Collins Campers, Inc., 697 N. 34th Street, Springfield, OR 97478,   FW
Contempo Vans, 9175 San Fernando Rd. -2051, Sun Valley, CA 91353-
2051,   MB, VC
Colorado Freedom Wheels, Inc., 11055 Leroy Dr., Northglenn, CO 80233,
                                                                                VC
Combi-Camp A/S, Herrestrup, Grevinge, Denmark 4571,   FC
Coons Manufacturing, Inc., 2300 W. 4th St., P.O.B. 489, Oswego, KS
67356,   MC
Contemporary Coach, Box 512, 64654 U.S. 33, Goshen, IN 46526-512,
                                                                        MB, VC
Cormorant, 730 Middleton Run Rd., Elkhart, IN 46516   MC
Country Campers, Inc., 130 E. First St., P.O.B. 435, Junction City, OR
97448,   MA, VC
Country Sales, Inc., 71049 US 131 South, White Pigeon, MI 49099,   VC
Cree Coach, R.R. #1 M-40 North, Marcellus, MI 49067,   FW, PT, TT
Crescent Cruiser Company, 2750 Hwy 66, S., Kernersville, NC 27284 VC
Crown Custom Coach, 7300 N. Lawndale, Skokie, IL 60026,   VC
Custom Coaches, Inc., Rte. 4, Box 354-C, Elberton, GA 30635,   VC
Custom Craft Vans, Inc., 960 W. Armour Ave., Milwaukee, WI 53221,
                                                                                VC
Damon Industries, 28719 Jamie Street, Elkhart, IN 46514,   FW, PT, TT

DMR Van Conversions, Inc., 204 South Cedar Street, Monticello, IA 52310, VC

D. M. Conversions Ltd., 12651 West Silver Spring Dr., Butler, WI 53007, MB, VC

Day Cruiser Corporation, 22838 Pine Creek Road, P.O. Box 2296, Elkhart, IN 46515, VC

Dodgen, Born Free Division, Hwy 169 North, P.O.B. B, Humboldt, IA 50548, MC, VC

Driftwood, Inc., P.O. Box 501, Goshen, IN 46526, VC

Eagle Conversions, 210 Smithonia Road, Winterville, GA 30683, VC

Edgemont Industries, Inc., 55484 CR 15, P.O. Box 1383, Elkhart, IN 46516, FW, TT

El Kapitan Van Conversion Inc., 5455 Rosedale Highway, Bakersfield, CA 93308, VC

ElDorado Motor Corporation, P.O. Box 266, 1200 W. 10th, Minneapolis, KS 67467, MA, MC, VC

Elite Coach Corporation, 8525 Telfair Avenue, Sun Valley, CA 91352, MA

Elk Enterprises, Inc., 25771 Miner Road, P.O. Box 963, Elkhart, IN 46515, VC

Elkhart Traveler Corp., 2211 West Wilden Ave., Goshen, IN 46526, VC

En Route, Inc., P.O. Box 1391, Elkhart, IN 46515-1391, FW, TT

Esquire, Inc., 21861 Protecta Dr., Elkhart, IN 46516, FW, MB, MC, TT, VC

Esterel USA, Inc., P.O. Box 4507, 30338 County Road 12, Elkhart, IN 46514, FC

Excel Trailer Co., Inc., 11238 Peoria St., Sun Valley, CA 91352, FW, TT

Estate Manufacturing, Inc., 22617 Pinecreek Road, Elkhart, IN 46516, FW, PT, TT

Executive Industries, Inc., P.O. Box 2100, Chino, CA 91708-2100, MA

Etnom Corporation, 53664 C.R. 9 North, Elkhart, IN 46514, VC

E-Vans, Inc., 3505 Brooklyn Ave., Ft. Wayne, IN 46809, VC

Explorer Van Co., Div. of Bodor Corp., P.O. Box 46, Warsaw, IN 46580, VC

Family Vans, Inc., 1260 RT. 88, Lakewood, NJ 08701-4516, VC

Fireball Manufacturing Inc., 8646 Sepulveda Blvd., Sepulveda, CA 91343, FW, TT

Fleetwood Enterprises, Inc., 3125 Myers St., P.O.B. 7638, Riverside, CA 92523, FW, MA, MC, PT, TT

Florissant Van Center, 100 N. Hwy 67, Florissant, MO 63031, VC

FMG Conversions, Inc., 524 Imlay City Rd., Lapeer, MI 48446 VC

Foretravel, Inc., 1221 N.W. Stallings Drive, Nacogdoches, TX 75961, MA

Franklin Coach Co., Inc., S. Oakland Ave., P.O.B. 152, Nappanee, IN 46550, FW, TT

Free Spirit Vans, 101 W. Park St., P.O. BOX 264, Alamo, TN 38001, VC

Fun Truck'n, Inc., 45 Worth St., So. Hackensack, NJ 07606,   VC

Future Vans of Flordia, 2569 25th Ave., North, St. Petersburg, FL 33713
                                                                           VC

Gardner-Pacific Corporation, 5415 Napa-Vallejo Hwy, Vallejo, CA 94590

Gene's Van Conversions, 2406 Hwy 92 W., Indianola, IA 50125,   VC

Georgie Boy Manufacturing, Inc., P.O. Drawer H, May Road, Edwardsburg, MI 49112,   MA, MC

Geneva Luxury Motor Vans-CTI, 910 Madison Street, Lake Geneva,
WI 53147,   VC

Gerco Corporation, P.O. Box 804, 305 Steury Ave., Goshen, IN 46526-
0804,   VC

Get-Away Enterprises, Inc., 1711 Valmont Way, Richmond, British
Columbia V6V1Y3, CANADA,   VC

Gladiator, Inc., 55135 County Road #1, Elkhart, IN 46514, MC, TT, VC

Getaway Recreational, Vehicles, Inc., 476 Route 17 North, Ramsey, NJ
07446,   VC

Good Times Van, FM 916 & Hwy. 110, P.O. Drawer 464, Grandview, TX
76050,   VC

Gran Prix Enterprises, Inc., 1581 93rd Lane, N.E., Blaine, MN 55434

Gran-ville, Inc., 2200 Middlebury Street, Elkhart, IN 46515,   MC, VC

Gulf Stream Coach, Inc., P.O. Box 1005, 29337 U.S. 6 West Nappanee,
IN 46550,   FW, MA, MC, PT, TT, VC

Granger Industries Inc., 1913 Main Street, Granger, IA 50109,   VC

Happy Times, Inc., Route 13-16133, Tamiami Trails, Ft. Myers, FL 33908,
                                                                           VC

Hawkins Motor Coach, Inc., 1610 S. Cucamonga Ave., P.O. Box 3189,
Ontario, CA 91761,   MA

Holiday Van Conversions, 1307 Karns Ave., Knoxville, TN 37917,   VC

Holiday Vans, 1902 East Michigan Ave., Ypsilanti, MI 48197,   VC

Holiday Rambler Corporation, 65528 State Road 19, Wakarusa, IN 46573,
                                        FW, MA, MC, PT, TT, VC

Holloway Debraal, Inc., 10711 Sessler St., South Gate, CA 90280,   MC

Home & Park Motorhomes, 75 Ardelt Place, Kitchner, Ontario N2C 2CB
CANADA,   MB

Homesteader, Inc., P.O. Box 900, New Tazewell, TN 37825,   PT, TT

Hornet Industries Inc., 24245 County Road 6 East, Elkhart, IN 46514,
                                                FW, PT, TC, TT

Imperial Industries, Inc., 21141 Protecta Dr., Elkhart, IN 46516,   VC

International Vehicles Corp., P.O.B. 424, 200 Legion St. Bristol, IN 46507,
                                                                   MB, MC

J & J Van, 650 Garcia, Unit #1, Pittsburg, CA 94565,   VC

Jayco, Inc., St. Rd. 13 S., P.O.B., 40 Middlebury, IN 46540,FC, FW, MC,
TC, TT, VC

Jeffco Van Conversions, Ltd., 4600 Gateway Circle, Kettering, OH 45440,
VC
Jet Force, Inc., P.O. Box 366, 26423 U.S. 6 E. Nappanee, IN 46550,   VC
Journey Motor Homes, Inc., 27365 CR. 6 W. Rt #8, Elkhart, IN 46514,
MA, MC
Joy Custom Vehicles, Inc., 1815 S. Peyco Drive, Arlington, TX 76017,VC
Juno Industries, Inc., 67320 Cassopolis Road, RR #3, Cassopolis, MI
49031,   FW, MC, TC, TT
KAJO, 3276 Fanum Rd., St. Paul, MN 55110,   MC, TT, TC
Kentron, Inc., 52897 Dexter Drive, Elkhart, IN 46514,   VC
Kim Tech, Inc., 1370 Mirasol Street, Los Angeles, CA 90023,   VC
King Manufacturing Co., Inc. 1801 Industrial Rd., Nampa, ID 83651,FW,
TT, TC
King of the Road, Old West Hwy 30, P.O. Box 2078, Grand Island, NE
68802-2078,   FW, MC, TT
Kingfisher Van Works, Inc., P.O. Box 777, Kingfisher, OK 73750,   VC
Kit Manufacturing Company, P.O. Box 1420, 412 Kit Avenue, Caldwell,
ID 83605,   FW, TT
Komfort Industries, Inc., P.O.B. 4698, Riverside, CA 92514,FW, MA, TT
Kropf Manufacturing Co. Inc., P.O. Box 30, 58647 St. Rd. 15, Goshen,
IN 46526-0030,   FW, PT, TT
Kustom Car Creations, 23350 Harbor View Road, Charlotte Harbor, FL
33950,   VC
L.E.R. Industries, Inc., 19475 U.S. 12 E., Edwardsburg, MI 49112,   VC
Lance Camper Mfg. Corp., 10234 Glenoaks Blvd., Pacoinia, CA 91331,
FW, TC
LaTour Luxury Vans, 794 South Broadway, Hicksville, NY 11801,   VC
Landmark Industries, Inc., P.O. Box 4731, 52684 Winding Water Lane,
Elkhart, IN 46514,   FC, TC, TT
Lazy Daze, Inc., 4303 E. Mission Blvd., Pomona, CA 91766,   MC
Leer Inc., 58288 Ventura Drive, Elkhart, IN 46517,   PU
Leisure Coach, Inc., 13659 Rosecrans Ave., 1-A, Santa Fe Springs, CA
90650,   VC
Leisure Guide of American, Inc., Route 1 Box 51B, Royston, GA 30662,
VC
Legacy Vans, 22932 Pine Creek Road, Elkhart, IN 46516,   VC
Les Enterprises Campwagon, Inc., 1170, Chemin Olivier, Bernieres,
Quebec CANADA GOS 1C0,   MB
Les Industries Apalache Ltee, 1025 Boul. Smith Nord, C.P. 565, Thetford
Mines, P. Que., CANADA G6G 5T6,   MA, MC, PT, TT
Lifestyle Transportation, Inc., 307 S. Pike, Bolivar, MO 65613,   VC
Lipps Industries, Inc., 53386 County Rd. 13, Elkhart, IN 46514,   VC
Luxury Line Motor Coach Corp., 5th & Ellis St., Colwyn, PA 19023, VC
Luxury Camper Vans, Inc., 28731 County Road 6, Elkhart, IN 46514, VC

Magnum Conversion Vans, 4411 Old Tampa Highway, Kissimmee, FL
32741,   VC
Mallard Coach Co., Inc., 26535 US 6 East, Nappanee, IN 46550,FW, MA
MC, PT, TT
Marathon Homes Corp., P.O. 1302, Pine Creek Industrial Park, Elkhart,
IN 46515,   FW, MC, PT, TT
MTI, Box 506, Industrial Parkway 200, Wakarusa, IN 46573,FW, PT, TT
Mark III Industries, Inc., P.O. Box 2525, Ocala, FL 32678,   VC
Midwest Vans, P.O. Box 263, Goshen, IN 46526,   VC
Mobile Traveler Inc., Box 268, R.R. #3, Junction City, KS 66441,MA, MC
Mobility Industries Inc., 37555 Willow St., P.O.B. 425, Newark, CA 94560,
FW, TT, VC
Monaco Motor Homes, Inc., 325 E. First St., P.O.B. 345, Junction City,
OR 97448,   MA
National Coach Corporation, 130 W. Victoria, P.O. Box 2309, Gardena,
CA 90247,   VC
National R.V. Inc., 3411 North Perris Blvd., Perris, CA 92370, MA, MC
National Traveler South, Inc., P.O. Box 6404, 2142 W. Broad Street,
Athens, GA 30604,   VC
New Era Transportation, 810 Moe Drive, Akron, OH 44310,   VC
New Paris Enterprises, Inc., 609 N. Harrison St., P.O. Box 556, Goshen,
IN 46526,   FC, TC
Newcomer Industries, Inc., 65095 Go-Re-Co Drive, P.O. Box 806, Goshen,
IN 46526,   FW, TC, TT
Newmar Industries, Inc., P.O.B. 30, Delaware Street, Nappanee, IN 46550,
FW, MA, MC, PT, TT
Northern Lite Mfg. Co., 7410 S.E. Johnson Creek, Portland, OR 97206,TT
Nu Wa Industries, Inc., 4002 Ross Lane, P.O.B. 768, Chanute, KS 66720,
FW, TT
Odyssey, 2362 S. Gardena St., San Bernardino, CA 92408, FW, MC, VC
Okanagan Manufacturers, 316 Dawson Avenue, Pentieton, British
Columbia, CANADA V2A, 3N6,   FW, MB, MC
Osage Vans, Inc., P.O. Box 718, Rt. 1 Twin Ridge Road, Linn, MO 65051,
VC
Paradise Vans, 2950 W. Catalina Drive, Pheonix, AZ 85012,   VC
Park Haven, Inc., P.O. Box 4025, 57974 Co. Rd. #3, Elkhart, IN 46515,PT
Parkview Mansions, Inc., 25883 N. Park Ave., Elkhart, IN 46514-5001,
PT, TT
Park Homes, Inc., 21746 Buckingham Rd., Elkhart, IN 46516,   PTD
Perris Valley Campers, 707 E. 4th Street, P.O. Box 788, Perris, CA 92370,
FW, MC, PU, TC, TT
Phase III Vans, Rt. 1, Box 269, Pike Road, AL 36064,   VC
Pilgrim Mfg. Co., Inc., 15510 Lakewood Blvd., Bellflower, CA 90706, TC
Play-Mor Trailers, Inc., Hwy 63 S., Westphalia, MO 65085,   FW, PT,
PU, TT

Prattco, Inc., 1st & Broadway, P.O. Box 126, Summerdale, AL 36580, VC

Qualico Enterprises, Inc., 1210 Nance Ave., Lincoln, NE 68521, VC

Quality Coaches, Inc., 52743 Stephen Place, Elkhart, IN 46514, VC

R.B.R. Corporation, 13301 Chippewa Blvd., Mishawaka, IN 46545, VC

R & R Custom Coachworks, Inc., 1126 N. Santa Anita Ave., So. El Monte, Ca 91733, MA, MC

R C Industries, P.O. Box 147, 16968 C.R. 38, Goshen, IN 46526, FW, PT, TT

Red-E-Kamp, Inc., 811A Space Center, Mira Loma Space Center, Mira Loma, CA 91752, MP, VC

Research Enterprises, Inc., P.O.B. 104 N. College, P.O. Box 56, Neosha, MO 64850, VC

Rockwood, Inc., P.O.B. 299, 201 Elm St., Millersburg, IN 46543, FC, MB, MC, TC, VC

Roman Wheels Midwest, Inc., P.O. Box 108, State Road 15 South, Bristol, IN 46507, VC

Royal Coach, Inc., 15730 S. 169 Hwy., Olathe, KS 66061, VC

Royal Diamond, Inc., 64654 U.S. 33 Bldg. D, Goshen, IN 46526, FW, TT

Royal Vans of Texas, Inc., 204 Texas Avenue, Round Rock, TX 78664, VC

San's Vans of Florida, 13712 66th St. North, Largo, FL 33541, VC

Sands Industries, Inc., 52161 US 131, Three Rivers, MI 49093, VC

Santa Fe Vans, 1801 Minnie St., P.O. Box 1633, Elkhart, IN 46515, VC

The Scotty Company, Rt. 2, Box 103, Ashburn, GA 31714, TT

Serro Travel Trailer Co., Arona Road, Irwin, PA 15642, PT, TT

Shelton Industries, Inc., 1802 Shelton Dr., Hollister, CA 95023, FW, TC

Sherrod Vans, Inc., 11251 Phillips Parkway Dr. E., Jacksonville, FL 32224-1571, VC

Sherry Design, Inc., 52918 Lillian Ave., Elkhart, IN 46514-9524, VC

Showcase Leisure Vans, Rt. 2, Box 174, Canon, GA 30520, VC

Sierra Custom Covers; 6205-C Enterprise Dr., Placerville, CA 95667, VC

Signature Van Corporation, 28591 U.S. 20 West, Elkhart, IN 46514, VC

Skamper Corporation, State Road 15 North, P.O.B. 338, Bristol, IN 46507, FC, FW, TC, TT

Sky Coach International, Inc., 240 High Street, P.O.B. 55, Washingtonville, OH 44490, TC, TT

Skyline Corporation, 2520 By-Pass Road, P.O.B. 743, Elkhart, IN 46514, FW, MC, PT, TT, VC

Southern Coach of Greensboro, 406 Pine Street, P.O. Box 20906, Greensboro, NC 27420-0906, VC

Spacecreators, Inc., 53293 Marina Dr., Elkhart, IN 46514, MB

Sportscraft by Coaches, Inc., 25954 Peirina Dr., Elkhart, IN 46514, VC

Sportsmobile, Inc., 250 Court Street, Huntington, IN 46750, MB, VC

Sprite North America, Inc., 211 SW 17 Street, Ft. Lauderdale, FL 33315

Stamina Industries, Inc., Rt. 2, Box 222, Howard, SD 57349, VC

Starcraft Company, West Michigan St., Topeka, IN 46571, FW, TC, TT,
VC
Starline Vans Company, 1001 East Main Street, P.O. Box 95, Albion IN
46701,   VC
Studebaker Motor Coach, Inc., 2356 Home St., Mishawaka, IN 46545,VC
Stuttgart Etc., Inc., P.O. box 855, Stuttgart, AR 72160,   VC
Sun Hawk Products, Inc., 67780 Van Dyke Avenue, Romeo, MI 48065,
MA, VC
Sun-Lite, Inc., P.O. Box 517, 54635 C.R. 17, Bristol, IN 46507,   TC
Sun Land Recreational Vehicles, 1320 S. Merrifield St., Mishawaka, In
46544,   MC
Sunline Coach Company, R.D. 1. S. Muddy Creek Rd., Denver, PA 17517,
TT, FW, MC
Sunrader, Inc., 22503 Pine Creek Dr., P.O.B. 188, Elkhart, IN 46515
Tech-Trans, Inc., 17090 State Rd. 120 East, P.O. Box 188, Bristol, IN
46507,   VC
Tern Industries, Inc., 508 North Harrison St., Goshen, IN 46526,   VC
The Limited Edition Van Corp., 53055 Paul Drive, Elkhart, IN 46514-
9229,   VC
The Van Connection, Inc., 2405 W. Geneva, Tempe, AZ 85282,   VC
The Van House, 1801 Cushman Dr., Lincoln, NE 68512,   VC
Thor Industries, Airstream, 419 West Pike Street, Jackson Center, OH
45334,   MA, MC, TT
Tiffin Motor Homes, Inc., 596 Golden Road, P.O.B. 596, Red Bay, AL
35582,   MA, MC
Torch Industries, Inc., P.O. Box 2268, 28384 CR 20W, Elkhart, IN 46515,
PT
Trail Wagons, Inc., 1100 E. Lincoln Ave., P.O. Box 2589, Yakima, WA
98907,   MB, VC
Trailmanor, 304 Church Street, P.O. Box 1010, Lake City, TN 37769,
TT
Tram Body & Coach, 5150 I-70 N. Service Rd., St. Charles, MO 63301,
VC
Trans-Aire International Inc., 52652 Mobile Dr., P.O.B. 2178, Elkhart, IN
46515,   VC
Travel Queen Motor Homes, 975 Morgan St., Perris, CA 92370,   MA
Travel Units, Inc., 28748 Holiday Place, Box 1833, Elkhart, IN 46515,
FW, PT, TC, TT
Travelcraft, Inc. 1135 Kent St., P.O.B. 1687, Elkhart, IN 46514,MA, MB,
MC
Triple E Canada Ltd., Box 1230, 301 Roblin Blvd., Winkler, Manitoba,
Canada ROG 2XO,   TT, MA, MC
Trophy Travelers, Inc. RR 1 Box 19875, HWY M-205, Edwardsburg, MI
49112,   FW, MC, PT, TT

Turtle Top, Inc., 116 W. Lafayette St., P.O.B. 537, Goshen, IN 46526,
MB, MC

Vacation Vans, Rte 4, Box 112A, Amarillo, TX 79119,   VC

Valley Vans, 11920 C.R. 14, P.O. Box 231, Middlebury, IN 46540,   MC

The Van Man, 1612 Cooling Ave., Melborne, FL 32935,   VC

Van American, Inc./Cobra, P.O. Box 124, 1402 Lincolnway East, Goshen,
IN 46526,   MA, MB, TT

Van City, 2708 Niagara Falls Blvd., Niagara Falls, NY 14304,   VC

Van House Coach, 25 Rt. 30, P.O. Box 427, Waterford Works, NJ 08089,

Van Masters, 1529 Alum Creek Dr., Columbus, OH 43209,   VC

Van Patton Vans, P.O. Box 1305, 22865 Pine Creek Rd., Elkhart, IN 46515
VC

Vanguard Industries of MI Inc., 31450 M-86-West, P.O.B. B, Colon, MI
49040,   TC

The Van Works, 325 S. Cemetery Avenue, Carlisle, PA 17013,   VC

Vans Unlimited, 1707 South Boyd Street, Santa Ana, CA 92703,   VC

Varsity Enterprises, 2821 W. Division, Arlington, TX 76012,   VC

Vehicle Concepts Corporation, Bristol Industrial Park, P.O.B. 427, St.
Rd. 15 N., Bristol, IN 46507-9998,   MB, VC

Vogue Coach Corporation, P.O. Box 2011, Sun Valley, CA 91352,   MA

Vyquest, Inc., P.O. Box 1727, Clifton, NJ 07015, FW, MA, MC, PT, TT, VC

Waldoch Crafts Inc., 13821 Lake Drive, Forest Lake, MN 55025, MC, VC

Western Recreational Veh., P.O. Box 9547, Yakima, WA 98909-0547,
FW, PU, TT

R.C. Willett Co., Inc., 3040 Leversee Road, Cedar Falls, IA 50613,   FC
PU, TC

Winnebago Industries, Inc., P.O.B. 152, Forest City IA 50436, MA, MC, VC

Woodland Park, Inc., 58074 St. Rd. 13, P.O. Box 1309, Middlebury, IN
46540,   PT

Wright Carriage Company, Whittle Circle, P.O. Box 604, Ashburn, GA
31714,   VC

Xplorer Motor Homes Division, 3950 Burnsline Road, P.O. Box 130,
Brown City, MI 48416,   MA, MB

Zimmer Motor Vans, Division of Zimmer Corp., 2801 13th Ave. E.,
P.O.B. 160, Cordele, GA 31015,   VC

Figure 1. This Explorer motorhome is only 18′7″ long, the length of a car, but has two double beds and an enclosed bathroom with shower.

Chapter 5
How to Choose and Equip Your RV

Camping on weekends and vacations is one thing. Choosing a recreational vehicle for use as a fulltime home is quite another. How can you make the best choice?

First, we'll discuss the meaning of terms because they are so often confused even by longtime campers.

A mobile home is a large house on wheels, with no engine. It is towed by a hired tractor truck and is installed permanently or semi-permanently in a trailer park. Mobile homes, sometimes called manufactured housing, are in a different category from recreational vehicles (also called Rec Vee's or simply RV's) and have nothing to do with this book.

We're talking about three varieties of recreational vehicles:

• Pick-up campers, which are small trucks topped with removable living quarters.

• Motorhomes, which are complete units with living quarters, engine and chassis.

• Travel trailers, which you tow with a car or small truck.

These broad categories break down further:

• A mini-motorhome is a single unit built on a truck chassis. Unlike the pick-up camper, which can be taken off the truck bed, a mini is a complete unit in which you can walk from the driver's seat to the living area.

• A fifth-wheeler is a travel trailer with a special towing arrangement.

• Van campers are customized vans, sometimes with raised roof and miniature kitchen and bath.

• Fold-out or pop-up campers tow as a small package, but expand into a full-size trailer once you reach the campsite. Some have canvas sides; others are hard-sided and look much like a travel trailer when erected.

Our own RV, in which we lived for up to eight months at a time during the years when we had no home except for the boat and the camper, is a mini-motorhome 21 feet long and 8 feet wide. The company is no longer in business, so we won't emphasize the brand of our own RV. We do, however, find it the ideal size for us now, and did even when we had no other home because it is large enough to provide headroom, adequate kitchen, and a bathroom with shower, yet small enough to park in any street or parking lot space that can accommodate a luxury sedan.

What we'd all *like* to have, of course, would be a 1500-square foot RV complete with attic, garage, workshop, basement, vegetable plot, and a couple of guest rooms. Any choice though, has to be a compromise among many factors:

• Fuel economy versus more living room and heavier weight

• Large living space versus driving and parking ease

• One vehicle versus two

• Your ideal versus a price you can afford

The RV that is right for one buyer will be wrong for another, even though both live aboard the year around.

The Pickup Camper

The pickup truck with a camper add-on is itself a compromise, designed for people who have trucks and want to convert them occasionally for camper use. They have not been engineered as one complete vehicle, so they're one of the poorest choices for handling ease, load distribution, and aerodynamic efficiency. You have less living space too, because the camper has to fit among existing truck components.

Although the camper can be removed from the pickup and left free-standing in a campground while you make the rounds of travel attractions, you're traveling by truck rather than in the comfort of a car. And the job of removing and replacing the camper unit, although not too difficult, is not something you want to do daily.

There are two significant advantages to the pickup camper as a fulltime home. (1) You'll have a complete and adequate home in one vehicle, with nothing to tow. (2) You'll still have a complete pick-up truck for use in business or for transportation.

The Travel Trailer

In travel trailers you have the largest choice among RV's in terms of sizes, facilities and layouts—and you can choose among many different tow vehicles too. On the minus side, travel trailers have one thing in common: towing. Driving hazards will be greater, parking more difficult, costs higher (turnpike tolls, insurance for two units, more tires). Your overall costs for camping fees may be greater too because car-trailer combinations can't stay overnight in supermarket lots or a friend's yard as easily as a smaller, one-unit RV.

A drawback to both trailers and pickup campers is that you must leave the vehicle to enter your living quarters—a nuisance on a rainy day. Trailers have the added disadvantage of being inaccessible underway. In most states, passengers are prohibited from riding or sleeping in a trailer under tow.

On the plus side, you'll have not only the most and best

RV living space, but also a tow vehicle that serves as your town car and extra closet. Small trucks used as tow vehicles can be outfitted as mobile workshops or even as minicampers for trips into the outback where you can't take the trailer.

In exchange for the trouble of towing the trailer, you'll have the advantage of unhooking it at your destination and forgetting it. This is especially practical for the fulltimer who winters in the south and summers at one spot in the north. You tow only twice a year, yet have a spacious, comfortable, and familiar home in both summer and winter quarters.

Price? You can probably get both the trailer of your choice, and a suitable tow vehicle, for less than the cost of a comparably sized motorhome. And you can trade off either as needed.

The Motorhome

Because a motorhome is a single unit incorporating both your home and car, it offers both the convenience, and the burden, of taking everything along for the ride everywhere you go. Well-engineered motorhomes are a dream on the highway, but the large ones are more difficult to handle in city traffic, on narrow streets in old cities like Key West, and on country roads with overhanging trees.

We chose our mini because we do not settle in for long periods, but venture from place to place. Because our rig is only 21 feet long, we can drive anywhere, city or country, and park in any space that's long enough for a Lincoln Continental. We've lived for weeks at a time in relatives' driveways, at friends' farms, and at places where we were on assignment as a writer-photographer team. When we're attending a downtown travel attraction, we can park in any city parking space or lot. After the concert or dinner or trade show, we just feed the meter and go to bed.

The disadvantage to having only one unit is that every little errand means taking off the umbilicals and hauling pots, pans, bed, and board to the supermarket, dentist, movie, or library. A little advance planning, however, can cut down on the shuttle trips. We shop before going to any destination, and we like the convenience of coming out of the supermarket and stowing things right away in cupboards and refrigerator. At sightseeing attractions, we like being able to come out to the parking lot to use our own bathroom and make our own meals. If constant hooking and unhooking remain a problem, you can carry bicycles or motorbikes, or tow a small car (which gets you back into the towing trap again).

There are always those times when one of you wants to go out and the other would prefer to stay put. But you can't. I've spent hours in the RV in a parking lot, sitting at my typewriter while Gordon had root canal treatment. He stayed "home" in the parking lot and read, while I went to an opera at Saratoga.

Another minus is that the price for almost any motorhome is terribly out of proportion when you consider the size of a *house* you could get for the same money. In 1984, the average price for Class A motorhomes 35′ and over was just over $65,000. Many people spend more than $100,000 for a diesel motorhome, and I once toured one priced at $375,000.

Too, you're not spending all that money on permanent real estate which will increase in value, but on a highway home which will suffer wear, depreciation, and road damage. Even a minor accident could wipe out an entire kitchen or bathroom.

Summing up, we recommend a motorhome if you want to be on the road often, a travel trailer if you travel more slowly and stay in one spot for long periods, and a pickup camper only in the special instance where you need a pickup truck anyway and do not want to tow a trailer with it.

Narrowing the Choice

Only you can decide which of the general categories is best for your fulltime RV home. Now it's time to talk about layouts and facilities. Unlike RV vacationers, you need space for books, hobby equipment, TV, tools, food, kitchen equipment, and out-of-season clothes. Somewhere you have

Figure 2. Just because a door looks like a door doesn't mean there is an opening for a person who is taller than 6′. Shop for your RV with a yardstick in hand. Photo by Gordon Groene.

to store last year's income tax files, the Christmas ornaments, perhaps a sewing machine or trout waders.

When you're camping out, you can put up with many inconviences. When you're living aboard, make-do won't do. It is in this RV that you will be weathering all climates, entertaining friends, writing letters home, perhaps making a living, going to bed with the flu, serving Thanksgiving dinner, getting dressed for church, soaking your corns, and storing your golf clubs.

Let's start with the bed because it's a basic. It's also one place where some manufacturers skimp because vacationers are willing to rough it. If you're on the tall side, be especially wary. Many RV bunks are only 6 feet long. Widths too may not be standard, which means you'll need custom-made sheets. Insist on foam at least 4 inches thick, or your bones will begin to protest. If you read in bed, make sure there is sit-up headroom and good lamps (or wiring where you want to mount some).

Early in your shopping, decide whether you need a full-time bed, or would prefer a dual-purpose bed that becomes something else during the day. Fortunately the choice of beds in today's RV marketplace is very good: twins, doubles, queens. Many larger coaches now have large double beds with walk-around room. Without it, you have to sprawl across the bed to tuck in the linens. In any case, check out each RV by sitting, standing, and lying anywhere you plan to sit, stand, or lie for many years to come to see how well you fit. Shop with a yardstick in hand, and never assume that a bed or seat or shower is people-sized. Try it.

In addition to trying the beds, it's a good idea to go through any motions required to turn a dinette or sofa into a bed. Don't just watch the salesman do it; don't let him dismiss it with a vague wave at the gaucho. If you'll be going through this routine night after night, you'll come to dread it if it's awkward. Changing the sheets on an overhead double with no headroom is an athletic event. And the beds in some van conversions are just seats that flatten out, with nowhere to tuck in the sheets.

You *Can* Take It With You

The good news for fulltimers is that RV's get better every year. The trend is toward more space, better utilized than ever. To more luxury. To more choices. And to more gee-whiz gadgetry than ever before.

When we first shopped for a liveaboard coach, it was a real problem to find one that wasn't devoted primarily to bunks at the expense of other conveniences. For the couple who wanted a large coach for only two people, choices were limited because accent was on how many a vehicle would sleep. Now every manufacturer offers a big choice of layouts — twin beds, queens, even kings which are fulltime beds in a separate room or compartment. Most of the better coaches have a convertible sofa in the living room, for the occasional guest. Although you can still find a 25- or 30-footer that sleeps up to six or eight, the accent is no longer on Boy Scout troops.

Manufacturers heard cooks asking for bigger refrigerators with larger freezers. To fit them in, they've had to steal cupboard space but that space is now better designed and holds more. Slide-out pantries hold more canned goods than most conventional cupboards, and you see everything at a glance.

The lack of countertop space is being solved with cutting board fill-ins for sinks or stovetops — a feature boat galleys have used for years. Fold-up shelves are used in many coaches, to extend counters when the cook has a lot of irons in the fire. Most of the better coaches have come through for several years with microwave-convection, often eliminating the conventional oven. Many cooks will applaud use of this new, dual-purpose oven.

Colors are more modish, softer, less strident than in the days when only rugged outdoors types went camping. Fabrics are less practical than the old vinyls, but more plush and homey. Furniture is getting not just handsomer, but easier to operate. Some of the new sofabeds work electrically, and create a smoother bed.

Still, you'll probably have to go without some of the kitchen appliances you take for granted in a house. Manu-

Figure 3. Even though you have privacy curtains inside, a windshield cover can keep your RV cooler by preventing the sun's rays from entering glass. Photo by Gordon Groene.

facturers will put in just about anything you have the room
and money to add, but it's rare to see a trash compacter,
washer, dryer, or dishwasher.

Buyers of even the most modest new houses now expect
more than one bathroom, but this is one design feature that
may forever elude the RV fulltimer. Even some of the larger
coaches have only partial baths, or bathroom sinks too small
for any useful purpose.

Becoming common now are built-in, folding ironing
boards which are found as standard equipment on many
larger coaches. Central vacuum systems too are standard
almost everywhere.

Some design features still need improvement. One of
the gripes I hear most often at RV shows is that dining
tables are so skimpy, even on some of the most deluxe
coaches. Some dinettes seat only two; others have a split
design which makes it awkward to have company for dinner
or for a foursome to play cards. On RV vacations, part of
the fun is to eat outdoors at the campsite's picnic table.
In fulltiming, though, you don't want to eat outdoors every
meal, every day.

I'm pleased to see designers returning to awning windows
after they were almost totally abandoned for a few years.
Sliding windows can't be opened during rain storms, and it
can get very stuffy inside. Awning and jalousie windows can
be opened without leaking.

It's in electronics that the newest coaches really shine
compared to older models. On the most expensive new coaches,
closed circuit TV comes standard, giving you a constant view
of the road behind. It's an option on almost any brand. Satel-
lite dish antennas that ride atop the coach, and fold down
when not in use, are available for about $5000 extra. Look
for cellular telephones to become a common fixture aboard
fulltimers' coaches soon. The dream of taking calls on the
road, almost anywhere, is almost a reality.

Dashboards have become fancier and more practical,
with a better view for the pilot yet more bells and whistles

than ever before. There are alarm systems, signals, electrical aids, monitors and all the other luxury items. For passenger comfort there is a $500 seat which has inflatable sections, to support the lower back. Just pump it up as plump as is comfortable for you. A new orthopedic seat which has 12 different adjustments to personal comfort is an option for about $1200.

Except for some streamlining, most RV's look much the same today as they did ten years ago. It's inside that the most dramatic and exciting changes have taken place. Today's fulltimer has more choices, in more price ranges, than ever before. There has never been a better time to buy.

Chapter 6
Making the Break

As the man said when he stepped off the tenth floor into an open elevator shaft, "Watch that first step. It's a big one."

The decision to put aside a conventional home and belongings to go on the road, and the way you deal with other people about that decision, is that first, ten-story step. In the days to follow there may be mis-steps, stumbles, and outright pratfalls. Just how many possessions should you keep? What should be sold? Given away? What shall you tell the boss, your friends, your neighbors — and when? Is this the chance you've waited for, to tell people what you really think of them?

Three hackneyed expressions make excellent advice now:

— Don't burn your bridges.

— Dont't go away mad.

— Make your words sweet because you may have to eat them later.

For many people, the big decision to go fulltiming comes at a pivotal time of life such as retirement, graduation, marriage, or divorce. For us, things gradually evolved. There was no great, beckoning opportunity, such as a sweepstakes win or retirement with a pension. On the other hand, there was nothing cataclysmic such as losing our house and all our possessions in a fire, to force us to make an immediate change in lifestyle. In some ways this made things easier, because the choice of whether and when was ours. In other ways it was harder because, like most people, we found it hard to give up the habits, possessions, and hard-won career of a lifetime.

Our first decision was that we wanted our parting with Gordon's job to be a happy one. We liked the company and are still friends with many of the fine people Gordon worked with there. We were fond of our Illinois neighbors too, and wanted to sell our home to nice people for their sakes. Gordon gave three month's notice at work, to allow plenty of time for them to interview and choose another pilot. We were, after all, in our young 30's and knew a similar job would be needed when our savings were spent.

We broke almost all material bonds, but others might decide to leave more doors ajar. You might, for instance, be able to get a leave of absence at work, lease out the house for a specified period, and put the furniture in storage. There are lots of advantages in leaving one cheek on the chair in case the music stops.

If you rent out the house it will be there waiting when you decide to come back. It will bring in income every month, and it will probably be keeping up with inflation better than any other investments. Besides, selling the house now could leave you with a big income tax bite that could wipe out all your profit. You may like this furniture better than any you could buy later, especially if antiques are increasing in value or are family heirlooms you want to keep for your grandchildren. Your library or record collection could be irreplacable. Or maybe you simply want to take off for a certain length of time, then start back exactly as you were.

Selling out completely has its advantages too. For one thing, you may not have to pay tax on the profit from your home if you spend as much, or more, on the RV. Check with your accountant. If the RV becomes your primary domicile it could qualify as a rollover, as if you'd put the money in another house.

After the house is sold you no longer have to worry about mortgage payments, tenants who run out without paying, repairs, insurance, and vandalism. We know one couple who were having a wonderful time in Mexico when they heard from a former neighbor that their tenants had moved out, leaving the house a shambles. They had to leave their RV, fly home, redecorate the house, and find new tenants. It took three months.

When you sell out, you have the money in hand to spend on today's fun. Besides, when you settle down again you may not want to return to the same town. If you sell the furniture, you don't have to worry about storage payments, fire, deterioration, changing styles, and mildew. And your tastes could change completely while you're away.

Our decision was to get rid of everything except a few family heirlooms and the pump organ Gordon had painstakingly restored. We had happy memories of starting our marriage with nothing, and then saving dollar by dollar to buy the things we wanted. We knew that, if and when we lived in a house again, it would be just as much fun to start again as it had been the first time. We're glad now that we sold out.

Warehouse Storage

If you've decided to keep some or all of your furniture, there are several things you can do with it. One is to pile it all into one room of the house, lock the door, and rent out the rest of the house. If you do, get a special insurance policy for your possessions. Your homeowner's policy won't apply if the house is rented out, and your tenant's policy covers only their own furniture and not yours.

Or, you could ask friends and relatives to take anything they have room to store. It's free, and you can get into your things any time your relatives are home. A trusted relative can go through your things and send you tax records or financial information you need on the road, or can sell your sterling flatware if you're stranded somewhere and need the money.

There are problems with this solution too. First, you have to move the things to Uncle Angus' attic or Muffie and Bob's basement. Then, when Muffie and Bob are transferred to South America, you have to find a new place for your things and someone who will transfer them for you. There's sure to be a wrangle over who owes what to whom if Uncle Angus' house burns down or if Muffie's cat uses your antique love-seat for a scratching post or if your sterling flatware is stolen out of Aunt Min's dining room. And the day may come when Aunt Min swears the lace tablecloth was not a loan, but that you *gave* it to her.

It may cost more to deal with professional storage people, but it is often worth it. Because so many people today live in small apartments, homes without basements, and other cramped quarters, there has been an explosion in the ware-house and mini-warehouse business. You've seen them in your town. Many of them look like buildings with row after row of garage doors. You lock your own warehouse door, visit your goods when you please, pay a modest storage charge per month.

Prices may be different in other areas, but one mini-warehouse here in central Florida offers rooms in 26 sizes, ranging from a 4' x 8' x 4' bin to a spacious 10' x 22' x 8' room. Smallest of the mini's is only 4' high so it doesn't have standing headroom, but it would be ideal for piles of boxes, bicycles, a motorcycle, or other small items. It rents for $14 a month. At the upper end of the scale, the 10' x 22' x 8' room rents for $75 a month including electricity on which you can run your own dehumidifier. Electricity isn't available in the smaller units.

Such warehouses may or may not have 24-hour security. Some allow you access only during business hours, and are closed nights, Sundays, and holidays. Usually they are well fenced, but your goods are only as safe as the lock you have put on your own door. When you're shopping for a mini-warehouse, compare not just price and size but access and security features and whether electricity is available for running a dehumidifier. And don't forget insurance.

Another form of storage is provided by moving companies, and we checked with a local firm that belongs to one of the nationally-known chains. They specialize in storing entire homes of furniture, so your costs begin by paying for pick-up at your home. This costs about $220 per room in our state (but could be more or less in yours). Your household furnishings are then put into vault-type plywood containers so they are warehoused in a module, separate from everyone else's goods. This means that your individual pieces of furniture aren't shuffled around each time someone else's furniture is retrieved.

Monthly storage is high. You'll pay $1.35 per month per hundredweight storage plus a mandatory $1.75 CWT per month in insurance. That's probably about $30 per room, and articles are insured for only about 60 cents per pound. If you want additional insurance, I urge you to get insurance for the full value of your goods, that's another 90 cents per $1000 per month. Then, when you want your goods back, it will cost full moving company charges to have them loaded on a truck and brought to your home.

Although the cost is higher, the moving-company warehouse is usually bonded, has circulating fans, and a sprinker system. The warehouse we checked locally loads goods at platform height, four feet off the ground, which means well away from the ground moisture. Couches and other upholstered pieces are put on special racks where they get good air circulation.

The biggest problem in any storage, but especially in commercial warehouses, is moisture, heat, and cold because few of these facilities are climite controlled. Make sure there are no liquids anywhere in your storage. We once forgot that a box contained an old bottle of medicine. It froze and made a frightful mess. Linens should be washed, even if you're taking clean things from the linen closet. Dry them throughly, and put them away clean. This lessens the chance of mildew and other atmospheric stains. They are almost inevitable in the driest northern attic as well as in basement or warehouse storage. Re-wash things every couple of years.

We once stored a few things in a mini-warehouse at a Florida waterfront where a friend's beautiful antique linens had rotted away in only a few months. We had less trouble because our linens were washed and dried, then sealed in plastic bags with a formaldehyde mildew product. The linens survived nicely, but the formaldehyde smell lingered through several washings afterwards.

Make sure too that all batteries are removed from stored items. We all use so many batteries today, it's sometimes hard to remember they are in cameras, clocks and wrist watches calculators, tape recorders, toys, flashlights and so many other items which may up in the odd storage box. When batteries discharge and begin to leak they can ruin the expensive item they are in and even the surrounding goods.

Secure Storage

There is another form of storage you may want to consider for items which are too valuable to put in a warehouse but too bulky for your safe deposit box: paintings, antiques, silverware, etc. For the name and address of a security vault company in the area where you want to store these items, write the National Association of Private Security Vaults, P.O. Box 238, West Lebanon NH 03784.

Making the Transition

Our situation was complicated by the fact that our boat, which was our first roving home, was 1200 miles away in Fort Lauderdale while we were shedding our old life back in Illinois. The transistion is much easier if you can buy and outfit the RV at your house before you sell it. However, it's as much a mistake to buy the RV too early as too late. Once you own the RV it has to be paid for, insured, parked, maintained, and secured against theft.

Once you start moving aboard, be ruthless about what to keep and what to get rid of. Even if you manage to cram in the potato ricer or your custom bowling ball, it will cost you fuel dollars to haul and brake every ounce. Clothing, books, hobby gear—everything should be looked at with fresh, unprejudiced eyes. It's better to sell your wardrobe down to the bare skin, and use the money to buy one or two versatile and practical outfits, then to start off with closets filled with uncoordinated separates and shirts that need starching. Still, you'll take too much. We all do.

Once you've bought your RV-home, move into high gear. We allowed six months for our home to sell. In your neighborhood you may need more time, or less.

Selling Out

We began by running newspaper ads for our largest, least-needed items. We knew, from the experience of others, that we'd get big, unruly crowds if we advertised that the entire household was for sale at once, and we didn't want a mob scene just yet. Extra furniture, the second car, the slide projector, and other specialty items were sold through individual ads, and shown only by appointment.

Gradually we gnawed through the inventory of our ten-room house, 2 1/2-car garage, attic, and basement in inverse order to our need for each item. Guest room furniture went first. Then bulky games and hobby equipment, the freezer, Gordon's drill press and radial arm saw, the dining room set; and the living room furniture. Last to go were the washer and dryer, the kitchen appliances, and our bedroom set.

During the final weeks we had garage sales every weekend, and sold hundreds of dollars worth of smaller items. If you're not a garage sale expert, go to one or two to get an idea of how it's done. The most common mistake among neophytes is that they price things too low. Forget what you paid for an item back in the 1950's or 60's. Many things are worth much more than you paid.

Be forewarned that garage sale stalwarts can overwhelm you unless you stand firm. People started ringing our doorbell the night before each sale; others showed up for a 9:00 a.m. sale at dawn. Fortunately we were able to price our things, arrange them in the garage, and keep the door locked until our advertised sale time.

It isn't fair to those people who observe your sale hours, to let others get "first pickings" early. Nor, we decided, were we so desperate to sell things that we would allow our household routine to be upset by these jackals. This is a nerve-jangling period, so keep your cool.

We discovered that it's important to have some kind of crowd control by roping off the yard, or setting up tables in a pattern around the garage or porch so crowds can't stampede your goods. Lock the house while you're out selling. With the kinds of crowds we had, things could have gotten out of hand.

Don't forget to start sale day with plenty of change. A carpenter's apron or big pockets help you keep control of the cash. If you keep all the cash in a box in one spot, it's too easy for someone to walk off with it while you're demonstrating how the lawn mower works or helping someone try on your roller skates.

Some other suggestions follow:

1. Put a price on everything. It eliminates confusion not just between you and the customer, but between you and your spouse or other helpers at the sale. Masking tape is cheap and easy for the job. Have a good supply of paper bags, newspaper for wrapping breakables, and boxes for packing large purchases.

2. Don't put out the entire household at once if you have as much as we did. It's easier to keep things under control if you put out only part at a time.

3. Beware of dealers who come early and offer a flat rate for everything. It may sound like a lot, but we made far more money by extending the sale and lowering our prices the last day.

Some Other Choices

Garage sales are a gold mine, but you may be wiser to

give away some items than to sell them. In our area, books won't bring even a fraction of their original cost. See if you can donate yours to a library and write them off your taxes at their real value. The same can be true of some antiques and paintings. We also found that men's suits that had cost $200 and more wouldn't bring $10 at our sales. By donating them to a charity, we were able to get a tax write-off.

Another choice is to hold an auction. It's painful to sell off bits and pieces of your life at a garage sale. By turning everything over to an auctioneer, and walking away until after the sale, you are spared the work and the sadness of selling. The price, however, is high. Auctioneers take at least 25 percent and, if weather is bad, your goods may sell for far less than you'd hoped.

Parting is Such Sweet Sorrow

No matter how you choose to unload your possessions, there will be difficult decisions to make, perhaps some argument with your husband or wife about what to keep or what prices to ask, and a real sense of loss and ambivalence. Steel yourself for it. Suddenly you realize how many good times you had in this home, how comfortable you were in that old overcoat, how much you liked the silly little lamp the two of you picked out for your first apartment, and how much you'll miss the doo-dads that caught the morning sun in the bay window.

In addition to your own bittersweet partings with familiar goods, expect some ugly pressures from other people. Relatives may get huffy if they catch you selling gifts they gave you. Friends and neighbors may expect you to give things away because you're breaking up housekeeping. Secondhand dealers gather like crows around carrion, prying for every price advantage.

This is a time of great mental, physical, and financial vulnerability. Be alert against hurts of all kinds. This is the tough part, but it's soon over. Now, let the good times roll!

PART TWO
Get Set

Chapter 7
Driving the Big Ones

"I'd love to have the biggest motorhome I can afford, but they're so big, they scare me." It's a common feeling.

If you're thinking of going on the road with a big trailer or motorhome after years of driving only cars or small trailers, you can start practicing right now. If it's allowed by your state law, buy or rent the mirrors that are put on cars that tow trailers. They'll be at least 8′ wide, probably a few inches more. After using them on your present car for a week or so, you'll have the feel of driving a vehicle as wide as your RV will be. You'll be pleasantly surprised to find that roads *are* wide enough, other drivers stay their distance, and trees and mailboxes don't jump off the curb at you. Almost automatically, you find that you are able to keep from driving these mirrors into anything.

Once you've seen that something this wide will indeed fit on most American roads, start thinking about length. On a straight road, you don't care whether the vehicle behind you is 30 feet long or 300 feet. As long as your mirrors will fit through the available space and you're going in a straight line, whatever is behind you will follow.

So far you know that you can tow anything of any length and of a given width down an interstate forever. Problems arise only if you want to turn a corner or back up. You're now ready for Lesson Two.

Even when you turn your present automobile, the space it requires is wider than the width of the car. The longer a vehicle, the wider the space it requires for turning. For extreme lengths, a vehicle must be jointed like, for instance, a trailer plus a car.

Any combination vehicle can be designed to track (follow) in the tire prints made by the tow vehicle. Look at baggage carts used at airports. Up to twenty trailers are towed by one tug, winding around pillars and through narrow spaces. You'll see the trailers track exactly where the tug has gone. This is because the steering geometry is built into each trailer to keep it in the right track.

Granted, these are short vehicles and shortness makes the problem much simpler. At the other end of the scale, picture a hook and ladder fire truck which is steered by the rear wheels too. Since RV trailers don't have steering wheels in back, towing any long trailer has to be a compromise between turning radius and length. Part of this compromise is that the wheels of most RV trailers are amidships anyway, for weight distribution. This positioning reduces the amount of space you need on the *inside* of a turn, but you have to allow more room at the *outside* of the turn for swinging the trailer overhang.

One problem with very long trailers is that you can't see what the outside rear corner is doing in a turn because it's blinded in your mirrors. But you will be able to see in the mirror what the inside wheels are doing, and you'll have to learn to gauge where the outside corner will end up.

A good way to learn just what you're facing is to borrow a trailer, or recruit a friend who has a trailer and hitch, for an experiment. A supermarket or factory parking lot on a Sunday, or a large church parking lot during the week, are good places to practice. For markers, use a few rubbish barrels or waste baskets, borrow rubber pylons from the highway department, or use chalk to make the marks you'll need.

Set up a normal corner like one you'll find on any highway, including standard width traffic lanes. Start with the car at various distances from the curb, and see just how much room you need to get the rig around the corner. Move just a few feet at a time, marking the track of the rear corners and the track of the rear wheels. This will give you a perfect picture of how wide you must swing around corners so the trailer wheels won't go up over the curb, and how close you must take corners to keep an extended rear overhang from intruding into the adjoining traffic lane. Both trailers and motorhomes can be put through such a practice session.

The other problem you'll have with long overhangs in a trailer or motorhome is with what's known as a departure angle. This is the angle between the road and an imaginary line from the rear wheel upward towards the rear bumper, clearing the lowest point in sight. In other words, you want to know what will hit when, in such situations as coming down a steep ramp onto level ground when the wheels are at the lowest point and the rear of the rig is still over the ramp. In some cases, and RV's plastic plumbing fittings will hit the ground. In other designs, a gas tank or other vulnerable spot might scrape and be damaged. If this will be a problem, one solution is to install a heavy steel roller to help boost the overhang over.

When you're in that unused parking lot, you can also practice backing up. If we're talking about a four-wheel motorhome, it will back up just like your car except that you'll need an observer in the rear to watch your blind spots. If your RV home is a trailer, backing up is simply an art you must learn. Some trailer parks offer pull-through spaces, but the time is sure to come when you'll have to back up.

If you've ever driven a small utility trailer, that's good news. You'll find that most RV trailers back up more easily, and are easier to control. The critical factor here is the length between the trailer hitch and the trailer's rear axle. The shorter the trailer, the more squirrely it is.

For us, the easy way to back up a trailer is to think of it as a complete vehicle in itself, then imagine that the rear wheels of the tow car are the front wheels of the trailer. Now, all you have to do is turn these "front" wheels as necessary to steer the trailer in the way you want it to go. Take your kids' red wagon and back it up using the front wheels to steer the back wheels. Now picture the front wheels of this wagon as the back wheels of your own car.

With this system, you don't have to remember which way to turn the steering wheel. You only have to turn the "front" wheels of your trailer (the back wheels of the car) in the direction needed to maneuver your trailer.

If you have a good imagination you can picture this whole process as you sit in the car looking out the back window. If not, cinch up your seat belt, lean out the car door, and watch the back wheels of the car. Turn the steering wheel whatever way necessary to make these wheels do exactly what you want them to. If you can just picture the back axle of the car as the front wheels of your trailer, you won't have to memorize any gibberish about turning the wheels to the right, to go left, and so on.

Now, while you still have this whole parking lot to yourself, learn to back up, park, make backward U-turns, and otherwise handle your RV with confidence.

While you're at it, strictly memorize the tightest angle that you can get between the car and trailer before something hits. Then always keep at least 5 degrees in reserve unless an observer is standing there to advise you.

Now that you're ready to solo on the highway, you have some nice surprises in store, especially in driving a large motorhome. For one thing, any vehicle with a longer-than-standard wheelbase tracks better, making it easier to steer and easier to keep on course. Also, any seating position that gives you an eye level higher than normal greatly adds to driving pleasure and safety, because you can see traffic far ahead of the next car. This, then, gives you more time to react to trouble ahead, as well as a clearer view of traffic signs, road information, and approaching potholes.

You'll also find when you're in your big RV that other drivers can see you better, and will tend to relinquish right of way. Don't use your size to bluff, bully, or take chances, of course. You could get your powder room sideswiped. Still, it's comforting to find that you can be seen readily.

Some of the larger units, because they are more stable in a straight line are, conversely, more difficult to maneuver in defensive driving. Also, you can't stop a big RV as fast as a car, so you should always drive with one eye cocked for an escape route if your traffic lane becomes blocked, as in a multi-car pile-up. When the road is clear, practice miximum-effort braking. There's no other way to learn just what will happen to you, to the brakes, and to all the pots and pans in your cupboards. When you have space available and no traffic around, practice rapid lane-changing. In general, know just what your RV can and cannot do and always allow for all the space you need around you.

We've talked about getting to know your RV's length width, and turning radius by "feel". It's also important to know your RV's height in feet and inches by actual measure. Underpasses are clearly marked. If you know your height, (make a label and put it on the dashboard so you can't forget this figure) you can sail underneath without stopping and sighting. One trick you can use for overhangs that are not marked at gas stations and drive-ins, is to mount a whip antenna on the front bumper of the tow car to the exact height of the highest point on your trailer. If the antenna scrapes, you know the rig won't fit. This idea also works well with pick-up campers.

Courtesy is always in style and, as a fulltime RV driver, you'll gain more friends for the RV community, and gain a safety edge for yourself, but staying ever-mindful of the other guy on the road and of his problems. As a fulltimer, why not just stay off the road on holiday weekends and let other drivers have their turn?

While driving a large and cumbersome rig, always notice when you are holding up the parade. On a winding road, don't hold up the bus driver or truck driver who has to keep on a schedule or the sports car driver who is feeling his oats. Pull into the first available rest stop if a line has formed behind you, and let them all go by. Your courtesy will be appreciated, and there will be just that many fewer vehicles on your tail if you have to make a panic stop.

Use all the old truck driver tricks, and any new ones you can dream up to add to your safety. In hilly country where there are passing lanes, plan ahead to get immediately into the slow lane before someone comes up on your right side. On multi-lane highways, pick the lane that is moving at the speed most comfortable for you so you don't impede others. Magnify all your best driving manners — turn signals, stop signals, headlight dimming, a flick of the headlights to show a trucker that he has passed you safely.

One last safety rule. The driver of the RV must be like the captain of a ship. Anyone else aboard can act only as an advisor. Observations are appreciated but quick, disconcerting orders only endanger everyone's life.

In the Campground
Many times we've seen an RV driver make a braying ass of himself by loudly chewing out his copilot for "letting" him back into an overhead branch, a sand trap, or a chuck hole. Tell it to the marines. As driver-captain of this land yacht, you're in charge. Anything that goes awry is, in the final analysis, your fault.

First of all, you'll call less attention to yourself, no matter how big a hash you make of your driving, by suffering in silence. If a 450-ton Boeing 747 can be parked on a pinpoint at an airport without a word, there is no reason why you and your crew can't also develop hand signals to communicate over the sound of an RV engine. You'll disturb others less, and look much more clever, because you've been smart enough to keep your trap shut while you miss the hitch for the forty-fifth time.

Figure 4. Hand signals clearly show the driver what is going on beside, under, behind, and above the RV during parking and maneuvering. Shouting is confusing and unnecessary. Photos by Gordon Groene.

Second, you as the driver are responsible for whatever happens, so you're wise not to blunder just anywhere your partner points. Before attacking the campsite, both of you should get out of the RV and look things over carefully. Notice where the utility hook-ups are in relation to your outlets. Discuss any special problems you want your crewman to point out as you maneuver — such things as an overhead branch that could scrape the air conditioner, a sharp tree stump that could damage a tire, or a seedling tree you don't want to damage. Make sure your copilot knows where you want to be directed, and where to signal you to stop.

During the time your sidekick is out of the rig acting as your director, he or she should also observe things that you, while driving, cannot monitor. Back-up lights and brake lights working? How about the tires? As they turn slowly, it's a good time to look for any cuts or unusual wear that might not be noticed after the vehicle is parked.

Campers are nice folks and want to help, especially if you are single-handing. Unfortunately, sometimes this "help" turns into a shouting match in which you find yourself letting someone else tell you where you can put your RV. Never forget that it's you who will pay for any damage. Manage on your own if you possibly can. If not, get out before parking and discuss where you want to go and what sort of advice you will welcome. In any event, nobody will be as careful as you will with your mirrors, your overhang, and your roof line. The stranger you meet in the campground could be the champion RV driver of all time, but might also be a recent winner of the RV Demolition Derby.

When you drive away from a campsite, don't assume that you can stumble out of bed, start the engine, and blaze off into the dawn. Even if you leave at exactly the same angle you arrived, there can be new obstructions such as a dog asleep under a wheel, a tool left behind, a forgotten hose. Walk completely around the RV before you drive away. Always. By the end of a year, you'll have a long list of accidents that did not happen.

Driving a big RV is new and different, and more than a push-button pushover. But it's a skill that can be learned, and one that can be practiced with confidence and safety. Go ahead. Drive yourself happy.

Chapter 8
Ain't Gonna Tow No Mo, No Mo

Let's say your RV home is a motorhome or pick-up camper and you're tempted to tow a small car for around-town transport at your destination. There's more hitch than one. Are there other choices? Most of us Americans are wired so completely to our cars that we can't envision life without them, but do you know what it really costs you to own and drive a car?

Your employer may allow you thirty cents a mile or more. Your accountant probably allows you the 20 cents per mile you're permitted by the I.R.S. The *real* cost of owning a car is, however, much higher.

When you're fulltiming, a car becomes a year-round liability both financially and physically. When you're on the move, you have to tow it which means more troublesome driving, more wear and fuel use in your RV, higher turnpike tolls, and tire wear to the car. When you're stationary, the car has to be parked, cleaned, serviced, and insured, and it continues to wear, rust and depreciate no matter how much or how little you use it.

On the plus side, a car is a convenience, it can be parked places you can't park your RV, it operates more cheaply than most motorhomes (however our diesel mini gets 21 mpg), it expands your storage space a little, it lets you go on errands without unhooking your RV, and it allows one family member to roam while the other stays home.

Let's look at alternatives. The first is to manage with no car at all, as we did throughout our fulltiming. Although it was sometimes a nuisance to unhook when one of us had to go to the dentist, we became spoiled by having everything with us everywhere we went. If one of you wants to nap while the other wants a longer look at the Van Goghs, home is no farther away than the parking lot. When we were headed to a dress-up occasion, we often traveled in our most comfortable clothes and changed after we arrived. Once we became used to the idea of having no car, we soon learned to do our shopping thoroughly so we didn't have to run here and there for the odd loaf of bread or quart of milk.

The places we missed a car most was for nightlife. We found we didn't go out for dinner as often. Sometimes, though, we *really* made a night of it by having dinner, seeing a show, and then sleeping right in the downtown, all-night parking lot. At carnivals, flea markets, rodeos, and other places where there are a lot of other people in RV's, it's even less a problem to stay for the night.

Here are some other alternatives to towing a car:

Bicycles. Some places, such as Key West and Martha's Vineyard, are very difficult to drive by car, let alone by RV. You'll see more, and have fewer problems, with a bike. You might choose to mount bikes on your RV to carry with you, but we find it more carefree to rent them only when and where we need them. That way, we don't have to worry about maintenance, lugging the bikes around, and having them stolen from our rig. The more suitable bikes are to sightseeing an area, the easier they are to rent there. Our bike rides around many destinations were the highlights of our stays there.

Public transportation. In some places we visit by RV,

we're better off to travel by bus, taxi, train, subway, or elevated than by either RV or car.

Tours. Why mope around strange cities with your face in a map when you can leave the driving to someone who knows not only the roads but the story of the city? We find bus tours invaluable for getting our bearings, and invariably we learn "insider" things about the area that we wouldn't have learned on our own. Bus tours are usually an excellent buy too, because the tour cost includes admission to museums, historic homes, and other attractions.

Shank's mare. Many times we're parked at campgrounds which are within easy walking distance of a shopping center, the beach, the museum, or other destination. We didn't need a car.

Motorbikes. These are heavier and more awkward to carry aboard with you, but will give you faster, easier transportation around campgrounds (where they are allowed) or town. Carrying a small scooter may make sense for you if you want it only for errands. In sightseeing areas it's usually easy and inexpensive to rent a motorscooter. Again, you have one only when and where you want it, and let someone else worry about maintenance and deterioration.

Car rental. It seems like such a luxury until you compare the true cost of car ownership to that of the occasional rental. We could rent a car one day a month for the same money it costs just to insure a fulltime car. Add up the cost of maintenance, depreciation, and repairs, and the interest you're not getting on the money that's tied up in the car. You very likely could rent two or three days per month, when you really *need* a car, for the same money it now costs you to own and drag one. Say you have a car worth $8000. If you sold it and invested the money at 10%, you'd have $80 a month — not counting savings on insurance, fuel, car washes, repairs, and depreciation — to spend on whatever transport is most suitable to this locale! My guess is you'd come out ahead.

A new trend in rental cars is the used car, often called something like Ugly Duckling, Rent-a-Wreck, or Poor Bob's.

A typical, medium size, air conditioned car in the '79-'81 age group costs $15 a day plus 10 cents a mile in our city, or $100 a week with 500 free miles. Collision insurance is included; your RV policy (check with your agent) probably covers liability.

New cars cost about $35 a day or $150 a week plus gas and insurance. In high-tourism areas where there are many car rental fleets in hot competition, prices are even lower. In areas where there is a lot of business travel during the week, tourists can take advantage of sharply discounted weekend rates.

If you do decide that the occasional rental car may be the answer for you, ask your RV insurance agent about what coverage you have when you're driving a rented car. Then ask the rental agent exactly what you are, and are not covered for. In comparing rates, look for mileage charges (most of the large Florida rental firms offer unlimited mileage), insurance add-ons, discounts, and whether they'll pick you up free at the campground.

Chapter 9
The Cost of RV Living

It surprises me that we are so often asked how much it costs each month to "get by" when one lives in an RV. There aren't any pat answers, any more than there are to questions about the cost of living in a house or apartment. All of us have our own definitions of luxury, rock-bottom necessity, emergency, splurging, and economy.

One way to plan ahead for what fulltime RV life might cost is to take inventory of how you spend money right now. A surprising number of expenses will stay the same. Your food bill, for instance, will be about the same on the road. Not counting inflation, plan on a rise of perhaps 5 percent in your present food costs to make up for two things. First, you won't be able to buy in quantity when items are on sale, because it isn't cost-effective to haul extra tons of goods around on the highway. Second, you'll probably stop at the most convenient stores you find in strange towns, and won't know, as you do in your home town, which supermarkets consistently have the best buys. Add on another 10-50% to make up for whatever gardening, canning, and slaughtering you do now which you won't be able to do on the road.

Figure 5. An investment in a condominium campsite may pay off, especially if you intend to stay put for long periods. This luxurious RV resort is in Palm Springs; others are found throughout the nation. Photo credit: Outdoor Resorts of America.

Sit down and list your food bill as explained above, and all the other budget items which will remain the same: life insurance, hospitalization premiums, time payments (car, television, the RV, that piece of land you're buying for investment), child support, alimony, care of an aged parent.

By looking over your bills for the last couple of years, you can average the cost of clothing, linens, liquor and cigarettes, magazines and newspapers, gifts, your annuity or a college fund for your children, church and charity, and other ongoing expenses and obligations.

You can also, by averaging costs over the past few years, make a good guess at other expenses: medicines, doctor bills, eyeglasses, veterinarian, dental bills. Not counting inflation or a disaster, these will stay about the same. Add in what you've been spending on restaurants, greens fees, a weekly movie or bowling, health club, organization dues, and other activities you'll probably continue while fulltiming.

It's true that many current expenses will stop when you go on the road: utilities, telephone, house insurances and maintenance, yard care, the second car, lunches at work, commuting, any special wardrobe needed in your job. But some costs will continue or rise.

With a few phone calls, you can learn what it will cost to license and insure your RV, to store your furniture, pay for cellular phone service, and to service any of your financial affairs such as home rental or business management. Guess at your telephone bills, based on how often you keep in touch with your family and business associates and how far away from them you will be. You won't have a monthly fee (unless you have a cellular phone), but long distance costs will probably be more than they are now because you'll be using pay phones and will pay extra for operator-assisted calls. Look carefully at discount dialing services. Most of them don't cover the entire nation, and charge a premium price for access to a long distance line.

If you plan to cover, say, 10,000 miles a year, get out the calculator and figure the cost based on so many miles per

gallon, and such-and-such price per gallon. If you get 10
miles to the gallon, and you're currently paying about $1.10
per gallon, you know fuel will cost about $1100 a year. Drive
20,000 miles per year in a 5 mpg RV, using gasoline at $1.14
a gallon, and the yearly cost will be $4560. Add in the cost
of oil, depending on how much oil you need per change and
how many miles your driver's manual says you can go between
changes.

If you'll be running the generator 12 hours a day, figure
out the cost of fuel at X gallons per hour, and pro-rate the
cost of the overhaul you will need every so-many hours. Laundry
machines will add another $5-$10 a week to your budget too
— another expense you probably do not have in your household budget now.

Think about the kind of lifestyle you enjoy. If it involves
quiet evenings with television or a library book, your entertainment budget will be very small. If you like top-name per-
formers, bar hopping, or pari-mutuel betting, entertainment
costs on the road will be as high as ever. In any case, you'll
want to see the most significant attractions, historic homes,
and best museums along your route so give yourself an allow-
ance for it. A couple of days at Walt Disney World and EPCOT
could cost two people $100 or more.

Other items too are guesswork. If you stay in commerical,
destination campgrounds, costs will be higher than if you
stay in state parks or park in a friend's back acres. If you move
often, and pay camping fees by the night, they're far higher
than if you pay by the month or season.

If you can fix everything yourself, keep a good stock
of spare parts on hand, and are reasonably lucky, you won't
have to budget more than a couple of hundred dollars a year
for repairs. If you can do nothing at all on the rig, have a lot
of complex machinery and electronics, and run into a string
of bad luck, your repair costs could be in the five figures.

If you're taking the long view and want to budget for
the inevitable, high-ticket repairs and replacements, save about
10% per year of the cost of a new engine, transmission, gener-

Figure 6. If you decide you must have household power whether or not you are hooked up in a campground, a generator is the answer. Costs can be estimated at (fuel per hour) X (hours estimated use per day) X (estimated cost/gallon fuel). Overhauls and oil can also be computed on a per-hour basis. Photo credit: Kohler.

ator, microwave oven, and other expensive components. You can go along for years without spending a cent. Then suddenly the curtains die of sun rot, the upholstery begins to split, the tread on your tires disappears, and the engine needs a valve job — just as your dentist tells you it will cost $2000 for gum work. If you have a reserve fund that earns interest year after year, these inevitable costs will be less of a shock.

The longer you're on the road fulltime, the more you'll be able to fine-tune your budget. You'll become smarter about economical driving habits, repairing things you never understood before, and cutting corners in camp fees. You'll know how many miles you get from a set of Brand X tires, what products work and which don't, and where to get the best buys on insurances and parts.

As you can see, there is a vast choice in an RV budget, just as there is with any other lifestyle. You can drive 50,000 miles a year or 500. You can eat boeuf Bourguignon or beans. You can stay in luxurious camping resorts or rough it in an unused corner of someone's farm. You can keep your RV in like-new condition, or let it go downhill and take your financial lumps later when it breaks down.

The full cost of the RV life can never be gauged in advance, any more than you could know now what it will cost to live the next few years in a house or apartment. Other fulltimers can tell you about their budgets, but their figures will have little meaning for you because we all have different standards and needs. The true price of RV living begins when you drive the first mile to start visiting showrooms, and it doesn't end until your last RV is sold at whatever profit or less. The cost in missed career opportunities, or lost income because you took early retirement, will never be known. What you *will* know is the contentment of living out your dreams, the joy of travel, and a bank account filled with memories that no one can ever take away from you.

See appendix I for a fulltimer's cost worksheet.

Rehearsal for Retirement

Although some of us take off for a life of fulltiming with no pension and only modest savings, with the goal of making a living on the go, the majority of fulltimers have a full or partial retirement income. If you're looking ahead to full-timing in retirement a very helpful workbook, *Ready or Not,* is published at $7.95 by the Manpower Education Institute, 127 E. 35th St., New York NY 10016. In it you'll find lists of questions to ask yourself about attitudes and goals, plus work sheets that will help you figure out what your retirement income will be and evaluate how far your projected retirement income will take you.

The booklet quotes the Bureau of Labor Statistics that the average retired couple have a budget as follows:

Food	29.3%*
Housing	33.6%**
Transportation	8.9%**
Clothing	4.7%*
Personal care	2.9%*
Medical care	9.8%*
Other family consumption	4.6%*
Other	6.0%*

*Should be the same for retirees who live fulltime in an RV as it is for retirees who live in houses

**Your RV costs should be a combination of housing and transportation figures

Let's say, then that you'll have a net income of $1500 per month from whatever pensions, rents, interest, savings, dividends, and benefits are available to you. Using the guidelines above, you'll be able to spend about:

Food	$110/week
RV payment, fuel, camp fees, Maintenance, supplies	$637.50/month
Clothing	$70.50/month
Personal care	$43.50/month
Medical care (including Insurance, optical, dental)	$147.50/month
Other family consumption	$69.00/month
Other	$90.00/month

If you can manage an after-tax income of $2000 a month, you can budget as follows:

Food	$146.50/week
RV payment, fuel, camp Fees, maintenance, supplies	$850/month
Clothing	$94/month
Personal care	$58/month
Medical, dental	$196/month
Other	$212/month

As you can see, much depends on the factors discussed earlier in this chapter. If you're paying a mechanic $12 per hour to do all routine maintenance and the occasional repair on your RV, it can cost hundreds of dollars at a crack. If your RV is paid for as you begin, your situation will be different from that of the fulltimer who has a three-year loan to pay off. If you spend most of your winter months in a campground at monthly rates, your over all costs can be less than that of the fulltimer who pays by the night or the week (but less than that of the fulltimer who camps with friends and relatives or who owns his own campsite).

Too, there is a lot of fudging that can be done within this very vague outline. Do dry cleaning, coin laundry, and shoe repair come under Clothing or Personal Care? Do sheets and towels come out of clothing budget or "other"? Do detergents and bug sprays come under Food if you buy them in the supermarket?

Both the Other and Other Family Consumption categories add up to 10.6%. If you tithe 10% to church and charity, as many people do, does this mean you have only .6% left for telephone calls, gifts to family, and admissions to museums?

As much as all of us would like to have slick, pat answers, it continues to be impossible for anyone to tell you how many dollars you can really count on day by day, and how far those dollars will go. Fulltime life-on-the-go is as unpredictable, as cheap and as expensive as your life has always been — but infinitely more rewarding than money can buy.

Chapter 10
Are You Insured?

You live fulltime aboard your motorcoach and have no other home. Picture yourself in one of the following pickles:

1. You golf ball conks a bystander and you are sued.
2. You carry the sterling flatware board, and it's stolen.
3. Your dog bites a child who is passing by your campsite.
4. You and your guests are sitting under your awning on the patio when your folding chair collapses under your guest.
5. Your safety deposit box is rifled in a major bank heist.
6. Your suitcase is stolen while you are checking in at the airport.
7. You sister and brother-in-law agreed to store your valuable Oriental rug in their attic while you're roaming, and their house burns down.
8. There's a fire in your coach, and your expensive cameras are totalled.

When you're living in a house, many of these losses and liabilities are covered by standard home owner's policies and you take them for granted. Even the best motorcoach policy, however, is not designed for the special needs of the fulltimer. You need a special, separate policy to cover the situations above, and other coverages which you had as a homeowner but do not have as a fulltime roamer.

Some fine legwork was done for me by Ruth Steel Walker, in the Public Relations of the Foremost Insurance Company. Her answers are based on the assumption that 1) you're a fulltimer with no other home, 2) that you have standard motor vehicle liability and physical damage coverage, 3) that you have personal effects in the coach covered for a specified amount and 4) that you have no other insurance that would cover risks ordinarily covered by homeowner's policies.

According to Foremost, you're not covered for the golf ball, the stolen luggage, the filched flatware beyond the limits of your specified personal effects coverage, the guest outside the coach, the rifled safe deposit box, or many other problems which could arise.

Consider two coverages, suggests Foremost. A Comprehensive Personal Liability (called CPL in the insurance game) policy or endorsement could cover your responsibility for someone who is injured by your golf ball, broken chair, or dog. A Personal Property Floater (PPF) should be added for valuable heirlooms, antiques, cameras, or other costly items you carry aboard.

I heard too from David A. Hurst, who is in public relations with State Farm Insurance. He also suggested having two extra policies: a personal effects policy which protects jewelry, furs, silver, and other valuables against theft, fire, wind, and other perils. The company suggest a comprehensive personal liability policy to cover those liabilities (the dog), the lost luggage, the golf ball) that your homeowner's policy used to cover.

David A. Scott of Alexander & Alexander which handles insurance for many members of the Family Motor Coaching Association, wrote me, "You are correct that (RV fulltimers') needs require special tailoring to compare with the coverages of the typical periodic traveler who also maintain a home or apartment insured under a homeowner program." Homeowner policies include personal liability protection but in addition, Scott points out, many individuals elect separate coverage up to $1 million or more. Scott included in his letter a copy of a Family Motor Coach optional Personal Effects Endorsement which won't pay more than 10% of such things as coin or stamp collections, jewelry, paintings, and other valuables.

"Additional coverages for the fulltimer (should be) discussed with the insurance agent providing the existing homeowners program," Scott recommends. "Ideally this should be done prior to making the change, to reduce the likelihood of gaps in coverage."

When you begin planning your fulltiming life, read all your insurance policies with new eyes and get concerned, professional help to make sure you'll be covered as fully as you want to be.

Storing Your Valuables

Your banker can best advise you about a safety deposit box and how to handle it. It's best to get one in a state that does not seal the box if any one signatory dies. Yet you probably want access to it for yourself, your next of kin, and perhaps someone who lives in the same town and can get into it any time for things you need suddenly on the road.

Let's say, though, that you want to store things that are too large for such a box: silver holloware, works of art, or a large coin collection. There is a growing group of commercial vaults around the country. Don't confuse them with mini-warehouses or furniture storage facilities which have only minimal security and limited liability. The new security vaults have fenced parking lots, closed circuit television, and other safekeeping features. Rental for a big, non-bank safety deposit box sized about 50" X 30" X 2' costs about $2000 a year, plus optional insurance if you need it. For a list of private security vaults in an area that would be convenient for you, write the National Association of Private Security Vaults, P.O. Box 238, West Lebanon NH 03784.

Recording your Inventory

Getting the right insurance policies is only half the battle. Collecting what is due you in the event of loss is the other half. Much has been written about the importance of a household inventory. Fulltimers need the same sort of inventory of their RV home to know exactly what is lost in a fire, or missing after a break-in or collision.

One way is simply to start in with pencil and paper to list everything aboard, and what you paid for it, when. There are also some shortcuts. You might walk around with a tape recorder, taking the RV one section at a time, describing each item that is normally kept in each drawer or locker. Talk at your own pace, noting details about when you bought the item, what you paid for it, accessories you added, identifying features such as scratches or nicks, model numbers, and serial numbers.

A camera is even better as a reporter, and the more adept your photographing ability, the more valuable your inventory will be. With a flash camera you can get a pretty good picture of the silverware. With floodlights, or artistically-used available light, you can highlight every detail of valuable items. Remember that you're taking an inventory, not a prize portrait. Lay out the silverware or your coin collection piece by piece, so each item can easily be seen. Go for completeness and clarity.

Black and white prints will tell part of the story, color tells more, and color slides are best of all because they can be projected as large as needed to show detail. One way to combine both the tape recording and the photography is with a video recorder. Focus in tight on serial numbers, pan across sets of silverware, catch a shot of Mom wearing her imported leather coat, line up all the appliances, all the time talking about details of price or serial numbers that don't show on camera.

One way to mark easily-lifted items such as your portable TV is with your driver's license number, social security number birthdate, or even some nonsense figures that have meaning for you. While these probably won't help the authorities find a lost watch or camera for you, they will help you prove that the item is yours if you ever get a chance to claim it.

If you have really valuable things aboard, it's best to have a professional appraiser. There are also professionals who specialize in doing inventories.

Once your inventory is done, date it and send it some- where out of the RV for safekeeping. Then make sure it's kept updated regularly as you add new things, get rid of old ones, or as jewelry collections increase in value. Although some homeowners policies have built-in increases for inflation, you don't usually get this feature with a personal effects floater—the policy needed by fulltimers who have unusually valuable items aboard. And, if you haven't priced silverware lately, you'll be amazed to learn that a single sterling table- spoon sells for almost $100! Even good quality stainless steel sells for $100 or more a set.

You can get a free household inventory sheet by sending a stamped, self-addressed envelope to the Insurance Infor- mation Institute, 110 Williams St., New York NY 10038. Although this easy-to-use form is aimed more at the home owner than the RV liveaboard, it contains important reminders.

In the "living room", for instance, remember to list the carpeting, curtains, drapes, wall clocks, and other items which came standard with your RV. Don't forget books and records, plants and planters, musical instruments.

Under "porch or patio" list those items you have under or atop your RV: grill, folding umbrella, chairs. In the kitchen you'll easily remember to list appliances and silverware. But what about the costly foods in the cupboards? curtains? lighting fixtures? the good cutlery?

In the bedroom there are books, a TV and stereo, perhaps a sewing machine, toilet articles, expensive cosmetics. Costume jewelry adds up, and real gold and gems have zoomed in value. Even the garage/basement page in this inventory has reminders for the RVing family: don't forget to list tools, luggage, sports equipment, outdoor games you carry aboard, lanterns and other outdoor fixtures you get out when you make camp, the hose, pet supplies, bicycles or a shopping cart, fishing gear.

Have you priced linens lately? Don't forget to list all your sheets and towels, bathroom supplies including electrical appliances such as the hair blower and razor, expensive medicines and cosmetics. Our bathroom is about the size of a telephone booth, yet we counted more than $200 in inventory.

It's also a good idea to have good, clear slides, a movie, or a videotape of the exterior of your RV so you'll have some record of its condition before any minor accidents. Take a photograph of the calendar date each time you update. Don't forget to include the cartop carrier, and its contents and other accessories, such as the extension cord, you keep in compartments which are reached from outside the RV.

It may be more painful to be fully aware of the extent of your loss in a fire or accident, but an inventory will help keep the pain out of your pocket.

Chapter 11
Getting it all In

Mountains from Molehills

Clothes, linens, underwear, laundry. How can you keep everything straight, separated, neat, handy, unwrinkled, and out of the way? The answer will be different for each person in each RV, but here are some ideas.

One of the biggest problems with most campers is that some storage spaces are big, gaping expenses such as a hole under a dinette seat or an unused overhead bunk. This storage room is spacious and is desperately needed, but it soon becomes a jumble of tangled bathing suit straps and unmatched socks unless you find some way to divide and conquer.

Plastic dish pans are cheap, sturdy dividers, and they can be stacked as necessary. In our camper we have them lined up on the overhead bunk, one for hand towels, another for his underwear, one for her underwear, one for his shirts, and so on. Dish towels and sewing kit are kept in lidded plastic shoe boxes, Larger, lidded plastic boxes, usually sold as sweater boxes, are handy for larger stacks of clothing or first aid supplies. Lids don't fit tightly enough, so I secure them with bungee (shock) cord.

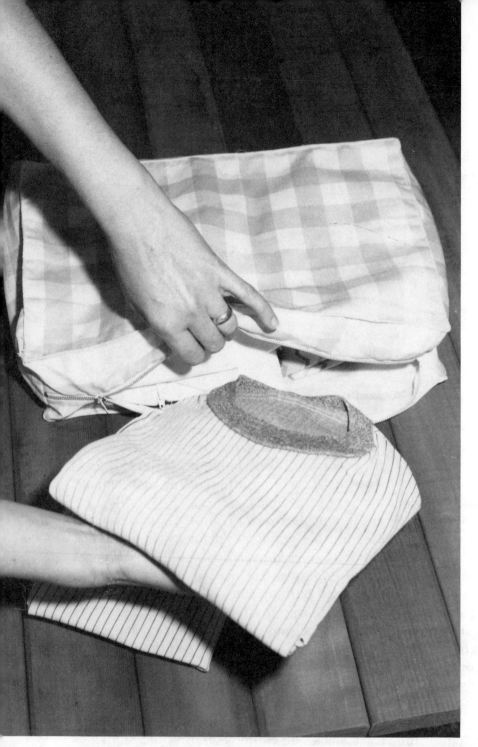

Figure 7. These simple gingham bags help divide and conquer. Transparent plastic sweater bags, sold in department stores, help keep clothing items separated in a large compartment. Photo credit: Gordon Groene.

Another type of plastic container is the sturdy milk bottle carrier-type box which is found in hardware and houseware stores. They're ideal for heavy use, filled with canned goods or spare parts. In specialty stores and catalogues, folding types are also available. These stow flat in a small space when not in use.

Another way to keep clothing separated in large drawers or lockets is to sew envelopes and drawstring bags from bright fabrics. Make one for socks and put a pocket on the side to hold handkerchiefs. Make the bags easier to identify by color-keying them: pink for hers and blue for his, or navy for under-shorts and red for socks.

Duffle bags are unbeatable for carrying almost anything, and they're especially handy for the RV fulltimer for storing out-of-season clothes deep in an unused corner. Sew a pocket or two on the side so you can find small items, such as mittens or wool socks, without rooting through the entire bag.

Soft luggage is almost always best for RV's but there are some instances where it's better to have a sturdy, weather-tight, rigid, suitcase. For instance, you may keep off-season clothes in the trunk of a tow car or in a rooftop bin, and find it's easier on the clothes, and on your muscles, to stow things in suitcases.

Carrying bulky ski jackets all year, even though you need cold weather clothes rarely? Instead of filling precious stowage space, use them for pillows. Lay out the jackets, arms across the fronts, fold them in half so the smooth back forms a pillow, and zip them into a pillow protector or corduroy throw pillow. Zipped into a pillow cover, a puffy quilt or sleeping bag will also look good and be useful as a pillow until you need it.

Visit the closet shop in any large department or discount store, and take a new look at the space-savers available. Shoes, for example, can be stored in stacked boxes, in hang-up pockets, or on the floor on a shoe rack. There are many styles of blouse and shirt stackers, pants hangers, and closet storage systems.

If you have a deep, narrow closet, look for Xtendables, found in department store closet shops. This is a telescoping

Figure 8. Collaps-O-Cart pushes easily over any terrain and is large enough to save many trips to and from your RV with food, laundry, clothing, tools. It folds flat and carries in a roof rack. For information: Knebel Associates, 5147 Burlingame Dr., Atlanta GA 30360. Photo Credit: Knebel Associates.

rack that mounts front-to-back in your closet, and is pulled out for easy access. One style holds hangers; other styles have hooks so you can mount accessory and shoe pockets on each side. All help you make optimum use of the amount, size, and shape of available space.

Keeping the load as light as possible, and stowing it neatly, is only part of the assignment for the RV fulltimer. It's also important to distribute the weight in a way that will be best for the vehicle's handling. Hang a big motorcycle on the rear of the RV, fill an overhead cupboard with canned goods, add a water tank or generator on one side, or hoist a heavy boat onto a roof rack, and you've upset the manufacturer's carefully calculated engineering. Mileage, cornering, braking, and maneuvering will be affected.

Parting is Such Sweet Sorrow

More than one fulltimer's story has ended on a sour note of crowding, clutter, increasing bitterness, and then a big blow-up between family members who were fed up with the mess. Yet most of us cut our teeth on the adage: use it up, wear it out: make it do, or do without. How can the fulltimer continue without collecting, acquire without miring down in possessions, fulfill without filling?

First, come to a full realization of what it costs you to accelerate, haul, and brake all those unneeded items aboard. One nationwide moving company now charges $1200 to move 3000 pounds of furniture from, say, New York to Florida, not counting insurance, packing, and other extras. To the fulltimer, this translates to about $2 every time you tote a five-pound iron skillet 1200 miles, $8 for hauling a 20-pound sewing machine through three 500-mile days, $12 to carry 30 pounds of canned good from Portland to San Francisco, or 40 cents per pound per 1000 miles.

While we can't make a direct comparison between moving van costs and RV travel, we've tried to make the point that nothing rides free—not those colorful rocks you picked up in the desert; not even that silk scarf that doesn't match any

Figure 9. Waterproof utility boxes can be mounted outside or atop your rolling home to increase storage capacity. Photo Credit: L.L. Bean.

of your outfits. It all adds up and, when you get your fuel bills at the end of the month, no one knows just which straw broke the camel's back.

Let's talk about ways to keep possessions at a minimum without sacrificing necessary food, gear and clothing, and some of the priceless books, cassette tapes, and keepsakes that are our homey anchors in a world that rushes by our windows day by day.

1. *Eliminate duplicates.* In a house it's practical to have one pair of scissors with the sewing, another in the kitchen, others in the office, still others in the workshop. One pair of good shears, two at the most, will do in your camper. In your kitchen at home you may have separate electric skillet, waffle iron, coffee pot, toaster, corn popper, ad inf. In your coach you can do the same thing with skillets and coffee pots that work on your gas stove.

2. *Give yourself limits.* When the galley's gadget drawer is full, stop buying gadgets. When the dish cupboard is full, no more plastic refrigerator bowls. When the food lockers are filled, no more cans and packages. Our only exception to this rule is when we are heading for a place where we can't buy food for some days (we have a few favorite hideaways). Then I may allow extra bags of food which must be stuffed in every available place. The bookshelf holds our ten or twenty favorites—whatever fills the shelf. When they are read they are given away or traded for new paperbacks. The same holds true for tape recordings. When the storage area for tapes is full, no new ones are bought until the old ones wear out, are traded, or are given away.

3. *Learn to cycle things faster.* One couple are avid magazine readers, subscribing to or buying a dozen each month. Each of them reads with a pencil in hand, noting on the cover any articles they want to clip or go back to. When each finishes a magazine, they initial it so the other knows it's now all right to start clipping. Only clips are saved, never whole magazines. Another fulltimer couple buy a newspaper daily. The old paper is thrown away, ready or not. Both know

they have to mark or clip as they go. All our food items are dated with a felt pen as they come aboard and are kept rotating, both to preserve freshness and to eliminate carrying around pounds of odd goods which "just might" be good in a recipe someday.

4. *What comes in must go out.* One fulltimer makes a rule that every new thing that comes aboard must be balanced by giving up something else. New shoes come in, an old pair goes into the trash bin. New towels are bought, the old ones become rags and the old rags are dumped. More propane capacity is added, fuel or water tankage is reduced. Once you have lived aboard long enough to know realistic limits, put the in-out rule into practice.

5. *Play the pretend game.* Pretend you were moving out of this coach into another one of the same size. What would you sell at the flea market? Pretend the coach was on fire. What would you save? Such imaginings force us to re-evaluate items and determine what is really important.

6. *Learn to be a little ruthless.* A good time to clean house is just after you've visited a packrat—and we all know a few. Come back to your own camper and look at it with fresh, unbiased eyes. Does it look lived-in or just untidy and over-stuffed? The smaller the coach, the harder we all have to work at giving the eye expanses of uncluttered surfaces to rest on. Sentiment can be carried too far. When we first sold our home and all our belongings, it was a bittersweet and often tearful time. We loved the furniture, brickabrack, souvenirs, scrap-books, lamps, and everything else about our big, ten-room house. Now we were off to enjoy the money gained from selling them and we were sure that, when the time came that we had room for new brickabrack, it would be fun to collect anew.

7. *Know when to quit.* It's not only cumbersome to carry around old medicines, stale cosmetics, and out-of-date fire extinguishers. It's dangerous. If it's worth carrying, it's worth carrying fresh and in full working order.

8. *Learn the joy of giving.* A volunteer worker at a used clothing center once told me the heartbreak he felt in going

through box after box of stained neckties, worn sweaters, holed trousers, and unmatched socks that had been contributed to his group. These folks needed warm, clean, wearable clothing. If you have items aboard which are not being used, don't hang onto them. Share them with someone who isn't as lucky as you are. Every sizeable community has an agency which would be glad to get your usable cast-offs. The more usable they are, the better you'll feel. Souvenirs too can be bought, enjoyed, then given away. Send them to some elderly or shut-in relative or friend who can't travel as you can.

9. *Water weighs about 8 pounds per gallon.* Although it's almost always the best practice to keep a good reserve of fuel and water in your tanks, it makes good sense to empty grey water and black water tanks as often as possible.

10. *Don't carry "hidden" water in foods.* Add it when you reach the campground. Dehydrated drink mixes instead of canned soda, orange juice concentrate instead of ready-to-drink, nonfat dry milk, and other concentrated or dried foods allow you to carry more food in less space, with less weight.

Traveling swift, light and free is what this RV life is all about!

Figure 10. Pets need a secure nest while riding and a thick, warm bed in cold weather when floors may be cold. Photo Credit: L.L. Bean.

Chapter 12
Your Four-legged Family

Deciding whether or not to take a pet fulltiming with you can be painful, and it's too often a decision based more on emotion than sense. We love pets—too much to subject them to the uncertainties and discomforts of a roving life. Our decision has been not to have a family pet. Our friends Sue and Don even elected to have an aged cat put away rather than have her adjust to a disruptive new life.

Before you dismiss us as sourpusses who beat dogs, poison canaries, and set fire to pussycat tails, let me give you a few horror stories. Champ is a big dog, too large to have much roaming room even in his owner's largish motorcoach. But he must wait, locked up, during the many hours they are away sightseeing each day. To pass the time, he sets up a howling serenade—which causes yet another and another campground to close their gates to pets. Puds, our friend's cat, has an inner ear problem which affects her balance, so she is miserably carsick every time they move on.

Sasha was a standard poodle who was asleep in the aisle at the time of the accident. Her owners wisely were wearing

89

their seat belts and were not injured. Sasha was thrown forward, breaking her neck against a table pedestal. Rover, the tomcat, wandered off from the campsite where his owners were overnighting. They waited and searched for three days. Then, hopelessly behind schedule, they were forced to continue their trip and abandon him.

One morning in Baltimore we woke up to find a German shepherd sleeping under our coach and, when we opened the door he began leaping against the screen door in a desperate attempt to get in. Apparently he had been lost out of an RV like ours. We delayed our own trip until we found a home for this magnificent, loving animal.

Mr. X, an adorable dachshund whose name we will never know, died of heat prostration while locked in an RV on a summer day at a southern tourist attraction. Many times we've carried water to dogs which were tied and forgotten in the hot sun at campsites while their thoughtless owners went to the beach or sightseeing for hours at a time.

Not all the negative examples have to do with pet distress. Owners can suffer too. A couple we'll call the Millers have two dogs, and the smell of their RV home could float a battleship. The Smiths, who are cat lovers, have the same problem even though they change the kitty litter often. Blissfully unaware of the stink, they both wonder why their guests leave quickly, and refuse further invitations.

The Browns are clean, responsible pet owners but they've been discouraged to find that many campgrounds won't accept them with their dog. Others require that the dog be left in a special kennel section of the campground, and still others require them to pay extra for their dog.

It's one thing to leave a pet alone in a spacious, familiar house where he hears the same sounds, smells the same scents, meets the same people time and again. In fulltiming, however, the animal who is left alone is constantly assaulted with new smells and sounds. It drives even the best-behaved dogs to prolonged barking. We know because we're often next door to such confused, dolorous, deafening dogs.

If you still want to take a pet fulltiming with you, despite the trouble to you and the discomfort and danger to the pet, here are some tips to make things more comfortable for both of you:

1. *Never wash the dog in the campground shower.* Even though you might be willing to bathe after, or even with, Rover, not all campers feel this way. Many campgrounds bar all pets because of complaints about this practice. Most dime stores carry inflatable, child-size, 36-inch swimming pools for only a dollar or two. They make ideal bathtubs for dogs. Use one outdoors, not in the shower room.

2. *Remember your pet's special temperature needs.* Leave lots of ventilation even on mildly-warm days. On cold days, even though the furnace warms the upper air you enjoy, the floor may make a very cold bed for a short-haired animal. Electric pet beds are available in two sizes from Patented Products, P.O. Box A, Danville OH 43014. Both work on household current. Thick and cozy, nest-type, non-electric pet beds are available from Cabela's, 812-13th Ave., Sydney NE 69162 or L.L. Bean, Freeport ME 04033. Both places will send free catalogues.

3. *An, I.D. tag is is not enough.* If your pet gets lost, it could take days and even weeks to find you via the tag. Search pet stores for a tag that has a capsule or pocket-type container for an address which can be changed each time you move — nightly if necessary. On it, write your name and the address of the campground, with your site number. You may also want to join Pet Switchboard, a clearing house which reunites lost pets with their owners. With your membership you get a pet tag inscribed with a toll-free telephone number. If someone finds your pet, he calls Pet Switchboard. Meanwhile, you call the Switchboard to tell them where to find you when the pet is found. For information, write Kathy Gilroy, P.O. Box 547, Lombard IL 60148.

4. *Check with your vet about the special needs of your pet in areas you plan to visit.* In the South, for instance, heart-worms are a cruel parasitic killer and special pills are needed.

Too, some areas of the South have a flea problem far more intense than you may be used to, so special precautions are called for.

5. *Train your pet to ride in a reasonably-safe spot.* If you have an accident while driving 55 miles per hour, your seat belt will stop with the car. Rover continues to travel at 55 until he hits something. And the something he hits could be you.

6. *Exaggerate your best good-neighbor manners.* Make sure other campers are not inconvenienced by your pet's mess or noise. Even though most pet owners are careful about covering pet droppings, they are less careful about letting male dogs and cats christen the neighbor's hubcaps. It's unappealing and smelly, and it causes rust. And if your camping neighbors complain, there goes another "no pets" listing in another campground guide. If you own your campsite, you may want to invest in a doggie septic tank, sold by Sears through their catalogues. The unit is placed in a 30″ hole, and it "digests" wastes as they are added each day. It comes with a shovel and chemical.

7. *Shop for special food and water dishes.* Your pets should have access to water most of the time, and a tip-proof dish for feeding. A nonskid table mat makes an ideal "tablecloth" for the feeding area. Cabela's, address above, sells an automatic dog-watering dish that attaches to a ½″ pipe.

8. *Keep both dogs and cats leashed.* Shop at pet stores and the Sears catalogue to see what's available in automatic tethers. Sears sells one that extends 15 feet, holds pets up to 80 pounds, and can be mounted on the outside of your RV or on a ground stake. The reel keeps tension on the line, preventing tangles. Through Sears you can also choose among several styles of scratching posts, to keep the cat from ventilating your RV's upholstery.

9. *Have the pet spayed or neutered.*

10. *Keep the pet, his bed, and his litterbox scrupulously clean.* Get plenty of air into your RV; you may not notice the pet odors after you get used to them, but others will.

Chapter 13

Minihobbies for Your Minihome

Almost all of us need absorbing interests to liven our "off duty" hours, especially fulltime travelers who may have to pass rainy days or evenings in areas where there is no TV reception, cooped up in an 8′ X 25′ cell. The trouble is that, because of space limits, familiar hobbies sometimes must be left behind when you go fulltiming. Here are some ways to help miniaturize your present hobbies, and new hobbies that might suit your skills and interests or aid your new lifestyle.

Radio. Although the CB craze is not what it once was, these radios still play an important role among people who make the highways their home: truckers, emergency services, RV drivers, and traveling salesmen. Even though most of the channels are silent now of the endless chatter that was so popular ten years ago, we continue to monitor our radio. Through it we can ask for directions, find out where to find a good buy on fuel, learn well in advance about approaching traffic tie-ups, and find out about detours that will keep us clear of accident scenes or construction sites. Recently we were among the first on the scene of an accident, and used our radio to call an ambulance.

For the most complete coverage, you might want one unit in the cockpit and another in your living quarters where you can use it when you're not at the wheel too. CB is especially useful when you're traveling in company with another RV.

Ham radio is to CB what caviar is to sardines. You'll spend more money on equipment, and must invest hours of study to get even the most basic license. To get into ham you have to learn Morse code and pass a written test on radio rules and theory.

In addition to spending time and money, you must provide a small corner for a radio shack, a good source of power, and an efficient antenna. What you'll gain, though, is a fascinating hobby for the entire family. It's not uncommon for husband, wife, and older children all to get ham licenses. You can talk to people all over the world, keep in touch with friends and relatives via telephone patches, help out during disasters when telephone communications are down, and have a world-wide network of electronic friends. Through ham clubs, you'll have an instant group of friends in every community you visit.

Square Dancing or Clogging. Both continue to be a national craze, and are particularly popular in campgrounds. Learn the steps and lingo, and you'll fit in anywhere you go. Again, you've learned an international language that will make instant friendships wherever you travel. And it's excellent exercise too.

Sewing and crafts. Many of us would be lost without our sewing machines, not just for the love of making clothes but because sewing and mending are excellent ways to save money. Three basics are important. 1. Keep the machine in a secure place where it can't break loose in curves and panic stops. It's heavy. 2. Allow some space for patterns, findings, and work in progress but try to finish one project before buying material for the next. 3. You'll need a roomy cutting table. Folding cardboard table covers are made for this purpose. Put one atop your dining table or the picnic table at your camp site. Folded, it fits under a bunk cushion; extended it gives you plenty of room to spread out fabric and patterns.

More compact, non-machine sewing hobbies include quilt piecing, knitting, macrame, needlepoint, embroidery, crewel, and huck weaving. Most good fabric and yarn stores give free lessons. Rediscover these old-fashioned skills.

Reading. When you're a stranger everywhere you go, it's impossible to have a library card. Still, we've always had all the books we want. Visit a secondhand book store before you leave and fill your bookshelf with inexpensive books. As each one is read, trade it in the campground. This is a great way to make friends too.

We swap book for book, and take anything that's offered. If it's a book that doesn't interest us, it can be used in the next trade. If your campground doesn't have a book and magazine swap box, make one and donate it. The sign "Take one, leave one" and one or two of your own cast-offs will start a happy cycle that will probably last for years after you leave.

When we want to do research for some of our writings, or just spend a rainy day reading fresh newspapers and magazines, we roll into a library parking lot and spend the day inside.

Handyman hobbies. The secret to any sort of workshop hobby is in having just the right place to work and a way to carry all your gear efficiently. We met one hobbyist who turned his tow vehicle into a workshop. It had a workbench and dozens of drawers. A good source of carriers, shelves, steel drawers, and other tool compartments is American Van Equipment, 212 Gates Rd., Little Ferry NJ 07643. Ask for their free catalogue.

One retiree who loved to restore antiques compressed his hobby into one specialty: antique clocks, which are small to carry and work on. His work case was fitted with little compartments for tools and bins for parts. When the case is open, it forms its own workshelf with a built-in light. When not in use, the case closes like a suitcase and slides under the bed.

We met a retired U.S.A.F. colonel, a fisherman, who set up his compact workbench to make lures and other fishing gear for himself. For sale to others, he made wooden name plates. On rainy days he sets up the workbench indoors. On nice days, he carries it outdoors to the picnic table. Dollhouse furniture, toys, jewelry, and model airplanes, boats, or trains are also good small-scale workshop projects.

Probably you've heard of Dremel, the company that makes the Moto-Tool that many of us call simply a Dremel Tool. You may not know, however, that the company makes a full range of serious, but miniature, tools: drill press, router attachment, table saw, scroll saw/disc sander, lathe, disc/belt sander, and a superb little vise with a swivel head. The entire arsenal will fit in a small trunk compartment, but will do work just as intricate and precise as you could achieve with full-size tools.

For years after we sold our home and possessions to live on the go, Gordon missed his workshop more than almost any other part of the past. Thanks to these Dremel tools he is able to have lightness, mobility, *and* the quality workshop that is important to him.

Order *The Dremel Guide to Compact Power Tools.* It's $7.95 from Dremel Division, Emerson Electric Company, 4915 21st St., Racine WI 53406.

Gardening. We once met a fulltiming couple who grew herbs, miniature vetetables, and greens in flower pots set in plastic dishpans. When their RV was at rest, the pans were moved outdoors. On the road, they rode in the shower stall. Gardeners can also enjoy sprouting edible seeds (alfalfa, mug beans, wheat). Another miniature gardening hobby is bonsai, an ancient art that requires much patience and artistry with plants.

If you own your RV lot, or spend an entire season in one campsite, you may be able to garden in your own lot, beg a patch of land, or start a garden co-op with other campers. We once spent a summer gardening in a North Carolina campground. When the harvest was ready, we all paid a token price for the vegetables to reimburse the camp operator for seeds, fertilizer, and the use of the land.

Treasure hunting. This one is addictive. You live on a hopeful high, believing that the Big Find is just around the corner. Metal detectors start at about $100 and take no more space in your RV than a broom. But, because the cheapest models signal all metals, you spend a lot of time digging up old shotgun shells and aluminum pop tops. Spend a little more, and you can get a detector that differentiates among aluminum, brass, and gold. The more you spend, the more sophisticated the detector will be.

We met one fulltimer couple who almost every day found something of value. At low tide near an old fort, they found a 17th century candlestick. Near an old Indian mound, they unearthed a BB-size gold bead.

Comb a popular beach on Monday morning after a big weekend and find coins and jewelry. On the site of a long-abandoned village in Vermont we found part of an old cook-stove, a 1910-style revolver that was a solid ball of rust, and a large silver spoon. As a practical tool, a metal detector helps find small items, such as a screw or tiny part, if we drop one in the grass while working on the RV.

One warning. Don't use a metal detector in a national park or any national historic site. If you're caught with one *in your possession* there is a large fine. When in such areas, remove the batteries and otherwise render yours inoperable in case a park ranger spots it. In any case, it's just good citizenship never to detect and dig in a site where qualified scholars might someday want to do archaelogical work.

Volunteer work. This is a tough one for those of us who have been active in church and charity because, when we're on the road, we're no longer able to be a part of a group or committee. If you're in each spot for a couple of months or more, simply wade in and you'll be welcome at the Red Cross, American Cancer Society, activity center for the aged, Meals on Wheels, or boys' club. Snowbird states are accustomed to losing many of their volunteers in summer.

Let's, however, look at volunteer projects that you can keep up when you are on the go constantly, as we were for ten years. One which we continue is to send postcards from all our exciting destinations to every shut-in we know or can discover — a former neighbor who is shut in with arthritis, an in-law's in-law who has multiple sclerosis, an old family friend who is in a nursing home, an ex-RV friend who had to settle down because of a heart ailment.

Almost everyone knows someone whose day would be brightened by a card or letter, and we keep adding names to our list. It's almost a thankless job, because few of these people are able to reply or even acknowledge our weekly notes. Still, it's a secret, satisfying way to serve your fellow man from wherever you are, with whatever time and funds you can spare, and without having to get involved with committees and meetings.

Another service you can provide right in your RV, wherever you are, is transcribing for the blind. Both voice recordings and braille transcriptions (which require a special machine and some training) are needed. Contact the nearest local agency, and ask how you can help.

Chapter 14
Continuing to Learn

Someone once said that the beginning of knowledge is the realization of ones ignorance. When we went fulltiming, we were confronted minute by minute with things we didn't know, and would like to: the names of new birds and trees seen in our travels, the real story behind the Battle of Appomattox or the Battle of Bennington, Indian history, foreign languages, art appreciation. Fulltimer's years are filled with exciting new sights and sounds, and you can double the pleasure by increasing your education to appreciate them all to the fullest.

Here are some ideas on ways you can enrich your travels by getting a college education on the go, or assure your children a college degree even though you continue to fulltime as a family:

First, write to the National University Extension Association, One Dupont Circle NW, Washington DC 20016. They'll send you a list of colleges which offer some sort of home study program. You work at your own pace, wherever you happen to be. Most good colleges won't give you a degree solely on the basis of correspondence courses, but you can earn many credits on the road.

After you have a degree course staked out, consider taking a CLEP (College Level Examination Program) test which gives you credit for things you already know — even if you've never been to college before. You don't even need a high school diploma to take CLEP tests. There are general tests, and tests on various subjects, each costing about $20. You can take your test(s) any month at about 700 places around the nation. A few colleges let you get your entire degree on the basis of these tests; some will give you credit only for passing some tests. Nor is there one "passing" grade that is accepted by every college. Each has its own criteria. For information, write College Board Publications, Box 2815, Princeton NJ 08541.

Some colleges give actual college credit for things women have learned through being housewives, mothers, and volunteers. Get a workbook called *How To Get College Credit For What You Have Learned as a Homeworker and Volunteer* from Accrediting Women's Competencies, Educational Testing Service, Princeton NJ 08541. The amount of credit you can get varies according to the college or university.

Write the U.S. Office of Education, 400 Maryland Ave. SW, Washington DC 20202 for information on what is called an External Degree Program or, sometimes, a university without walls. It's only available in certain places, but it means you can build towards a degree without setting a foot on a campus. The program puts together tests, your former college credits, credit for jobs you've held, mail study courses, and other factors. The External Degree Program can be found in New York, New Jersey, Connecticut, Florida, Illinois, Ohio, and West Virginia. In the West, it's available only in California.

Another non-campus study program is hosted by Antioch College in cooperation with thirty other institutions. You can take as long as you want in amassing courses, CLEP tests, mail order courses, and other credits to get a degree from one of the participating schools.

Television courses are another way to earn college credits. They may not be practical when you're constantly on the go because it's difficult to pull in the same television channel as you move. Although a course may be broadcast by various stations, you may miss some episodes and see others twice, because of varying schedules among different stations. You also have to be lucky enough to find the right channel at the right time each time you raise your antenna in a new campground. Still, televised college courses are an ideal way to get college credit if you'll be parked in one spot long enough to complete them. The time is almost here when you can tailor your own television education, through playing tapes on your own video cassette recorder, but I don't know of any program that has been formalized yet. You can, however, already buy video tapes on almost any topic.

Computers play a major part in higher education these days, and now there is TeleLearning which allows you to go to one of four colleges via computer and telephone modem. The credits earned here are accepted at 1800 universities. For information, write TeleLearning Systems Inc., 505 Beach St., San Francisco CA 94133.

Thanks to the growth in importance of the junior college, even smaller communities now have some sort of college program. A good place to start on campus is with the Director of Continuing Education. Sometimes courses offered in this department are shorter than a semester; sometimes they don't give college credit. Their advantage is that they are designed for the older student, the sometime student, the student whose needs—like the fulltimer's—are special.

Summer courses are another way to add to your college credits, especially if there is a special area where you want to spend your summer anyway. Some colleges and universities also have extension courses, such as a year in Europe or a semester on an archaelogical dig. Conditions and credits vary.

Any time you're taking college-level courses with the aim of an eventual degree, make sure there is credit, that the credit will apply towards a degree, and that it can be transferred to the college that will be awarding your degree. Not all colleges accept credits from all other colleges. By planning in advance, with a trained counselor, you'll earn that degree faster and cheaper.

Perhaps you've spent all your life as a teacher and now want a degree in history. You're a lawyer, but fulltiming has piqued your interest in forest management. You're a farmer but while fulltiming you've become fascinated by American history. Getting a degree—whether it's your first or your fifth—can add purpose, direction, and a new dimension to the life of the fulltime roamer.

Correspondence Courses for Adults

Not all fulltimers are retired. For some, RV fulltiming is a time of rest and reassessment between careers, or a last-fling adventure before settling down to a 9-5 life. Correspondence courses are a way for mature adults to learn new skills, and for young adults to continue their educations beyond high school.

Designed primarily for stay-at-homes who want to study at night after putting in a full day on the job, correspondence courses are ideal for the fulltimer because they come in the mail, chasing you down wherever you choose to wander. The secret is to get qualified instruction from accredited schools so you'll end up with a skill, not a scam. The National Home Study Council lists almost 100 accredited correspondence schools, your guarantee that the school has well-qualified faculty and other requisites.

Write to the National Home Study Council at 1601 18th St. NW, Washington DC 20009 and get their free folder which lists accredited home study schools. Then follow up by contacting those schools that specialize in subjects that interest you, to get specific details of cost, course content, and what diplomas or licenses will be awarded.

One of the most popular study subjects today is computers, taught by one of the busiest of the correspondence schools, the National Radio Institute which has about 50,000 students. In a typical NRI microcomputer course you'll pay $2500 tuition over three years, get 45 lessons, and receive ten electronics kits including a computer you build yourself.

What can you study by mail? Courses cover the entire cirriculum from accounting to zookeeping. Especially popular are things having to do with the arts such as painting, design, creative writing, photography, fashion, interior decorating; and with technical topics such as mechanics and electronics. Some home study courses lead to a college degree; others get you a certificate or diploma that may or may not impress an employer; still others prepare you to take state or federal tests for the license(s) needed in some lines of work.

Who makes a good correspondence school candidate? You have to be a self-starter, able to discipline yourself to study at least three or four hours a week. You also have to have the money for the course, although most have some sort of time-payment plan. And you should have the support of your spouse or partner who understands that, during certain hours of the week, you have to have a quiet place in the coach to study, build your projects, or whatever.

What does NHSC accreditation mean? It assures that a member school has competent faculty, has courses which are up-to-date and are educationally sound, that students are screened, that it advertises truthfully, and that it is financially sound. Every approved school has been inspected, has submitted its materials for review, and is re-examined every five years.

Where can turnpike tutoring lead you? It can allow your children to continue to travel with you as they pursue their educations after high school. It can take you back to your former career better prepared, or trained to a higher level than before. It can take you back to your hometown ready to enter a new career as a legal assistant or medical record technologist. It can prepare you to set up your own business in something like a doll hospital, gun repair shop, or jewelry design, so you can settle for keeps in a place found in your travels. It can launch you on a lifelong hobby in radio, writing, or music appreciation. It can give you a volunteer skill such as working with deaf or blind children. It can make you more independent in your fulltiming life, by teaching you to repair your coach's mechanical, plumbing, electrical, and electronic components.

Whether we plan it to be or not, life is an endless learning process. Thanks to home study courses, you can give focus and purpose to the studies that will make your fulltiming life richer in every way.

For some people time always flashes by so fast, the days are too short for all the activities they have planned. For some, RV-ing itself provides a nonstop panorama of friends to chat with and sights to see. But for others, time can sometimes hang heavy in the cramped quarters of the RV life.

If your rainy days are too quiet, the road too long, the hours too boring, don't blame the RV life! Look on these times as empty vessels you can pour full of pleasure as soon as you find just the right hobby to fit your interests and the space available.

It's true that the fulltime RV life slams the door on your roomy workshop or spacious sewing room. But other doors swing open, as soon as you find the key. There is one for all of us.

Chapter 15
Making a Living on the Go

Not everyone who lives aboard fulltime has a retirement income, and not everyone who has a retirement income can live on it. Some people make all or part of their living on the go despite the obvious difficulties. Others live on the go because their careers require frequent moves (heavy construction, carnival work, arts and crafts, research, et al.) Let's list some ways you can make a living, or add to your income, without settling down behind a picket fence and a row of rose bushes.

First, don't hit the road until you have some idea of how you'll support yourself. We've met some restless, job-weary people who felt trapped and who were sure that untold fortunes waited around the next bend, in the next community, in the next state. They were ready to tell the boss what they thought of him, stalk off the job, and begin fulltiming immediately. Mobility is not a guarantee of money, any more than stability is. If you're not a self-starter, you're far better off working for The Man.

105

A leading, Washington-based travel photographer told us the formula he tells other people who ask him about freelancing. "Work as hard as you can at your present job, and at your freelancing," he says. "Then, when your freelance income reaches 50% of your salary, you're fairly safe in cutting the cord and going fulltime. Your income will take a dip at first, but when you quit your job you'll also have more time to spend on developing your own business."

We also have a formula when people ask us about living on checks from magazine articles. It is to have enough money to live on for six months. By the end of that time, you'll know if you can make it as a freelance writer. A very successful romance writer continues to work two days a week as a secretary. "I thought there would be instant riches," she says. "I didn't realize that, even if your books are accepted, there is a long time lag before you have enough money coming in to survive on."

In our chapter about the cost of fulltime RV living, we explained how to figure in advance what some of your expenses will be. This is especially important if you're not yet at retirement age and must continue to make a living on the road. Besides not having a regular salary each month, you'll also have to see to your own health insurance, IRA, any materials or uniforms needed in your line of work, and perhaps income protection insurance. As an independent contractor you won't qualify in most states for workman's compensation or unemployment insurance.

There are many ways to live by your wits. We've met people, well educated people who could get white collar jobs, who picked apples or oranges, cleaned toilets in campgrounds, chopped wood, and did other lowly jobs. They didn't mind because the money enabled them to keep following their own rainbow.

If you do have a particular skill, it will probably pay to keep the tools of your trade with you. Engine tools, a chain saw, refrigeration gauges, a heavy duty sewing machine, upholstery tools, and woodworking tools are just a few of the aids which are small enough to be portable yet provide special skills that are in demand everywhere.

There has hardly been a time when we were working on our RV, tools spread around us, that someone didn't come over and ask for help with this or that. For those who need work, such conversations develop into profitable jobs such as overhauling a generator, checking out a cranky air conditioning system, fixing a faucet, adding a light fixture, or installing a water filter. The key is to have a cushion of savings so you can let such jobs come to you in due course. When you're new in a campground, people want to look you over and take your measure before trusting you with a job. And you need to manage the conversation so it's understood you have to charge for your services.

Some professions require almost no baggage. If you're a qualified teacher, for example, you might advertise for tutoring jobs while you're in a southern town for the winter. You'll use the students' books and can purchase other teaching aids as needed. Or, offer to give music lessons in the pupil's home, on the pupil's instrument. Buy music as it's needed.

We met one young woman whose marriage had dissolved just after she and her husband completed a two-year wildlife research project. Nearly broke, she took off in her van camper with several carousels of slides taken during those years. As she traveled up the east coast, she approached service clubs in each city (Lions, Elks, Kiwanis, churches) and offered to put on her slide lecture for a percentage of the gross. After seeing a few minutes of her show, they realized that she had a riveting, unique entertainment to offer. The clubs made money for their good works, and she cleared as much as $2000 a night.

Flea markets and crafts fairs can be a bonanza *if* you have a skill that's in demand and is not done to death. One fulltimer we met is very talented in making soft sculpture items, but she makes only unusual designs (geese are currently in vogue, Cabbage Patch-type dolls are waning). Another makes big, bright, soft-sculpture letters. At crafts fairs, she can easily assemble a child's name and sell it for so-much a letter.

An investment in child-size umbrellas pays off for a full-timer we met at a sidewalk art show in Georgia. The colorful, ruffle-trimmed parasols cost her about $2 each, wholesale, and she can easily stow 2-300 of them in her motorhome's rooftop carrier. She uses fabric paints to decorate them with designs and the name of the child, and sells them for $8 and $10. Her husband, retired from the Air Force, has router equipment which he uses to make wood name boards which are popular at campsites. On some weekends, he takes $500 in orders.

Neither of these people has an uncommon skill. Many people are clever with paints or woodworking tools. What makes their crafts a success is that they carve off a special segment of the market for themselves. Specialize. We know one fulltimer who sells only hats. Another sells emblems at camping rallies. Another sells only fishing lures. Some work for RV awning companies or sell some other piece of RV equipment using their own RV's as showrooms.

Sewing

A few years ago we met a fulltimer who travels by himself. When his funds get low, he gets out his heavy-duty sewing machine and begins taking orders for special awnings, up-holstery, canvas cargo covers, windshield covers, deck chair seat replacements, spare tire covers, and other heavy items. One of his most profitable items is a set of simple awnings that he put on his own trailer to shade the tires when he's parked. Others are always asking about them, and are quick to place orders.

His machine is a British-made Read, a brand that has long been the choice of round-the-world sailors. It can handle the heaviest sail fabrics, and operates on either household current or by hand. For information about Read machine, write Cook Marine Products, 101 Rowayton Ave., Rowayton CT 06853.

Figure 11. One way to supplement ones income on the go is to represent an awning maker or other line of RV equipment. Show it off in campgrounds on your own RV, and take orders. Photo Credit: Komfort.

An older woman uses her portable, household-type sewing machine to pick up pin money to supplement her husband's government pension. On nice days, she sets up the machine on the picnic table outside their motorhome, and starts hemming a skirt or shortening a pair of trousers. People stop by to chat, and she spreads the word that she's available to do mending and alterations. Her prices seem low, but she can clear $10-$12 per hour.

Upholstery

This is another area where specializing pays off. Our young friends live in their converted truck, which is an excellent showcase for their work. They have a heavy duty sewing machine, and basic upholstering supplies which they use to re-cover bucket seats or convertible RV sofas, replace worn overheads, make spare tire covers, and otherwise drum up campground business.

Campground Helpers

The ads usually read something like this, "Couple wanted for light handyman and cleaning chores around campground. Free site rent; some salary possible." For many fulltimers, a free campsite is well worth exchanging so-many hours per week (depending on the cost of campsites in this area and the value you place on your own time). We never wanted to get tied down to such a job, but were often told to "forget" the camping fee because Gordon had done some fix-up task as a favor to the campground owner.

Camping Clubs

Many clubs are small groups of like-minded people who band together for fellowship, without a lot of complicated bylaws and meetings. Others are vast organizations with tens of thousands of members, and large staffs. Such organizations need coordinators, evaluators, and salesmen of all sorts. In many cases, the fulltimer is the ideal person for such jobs. Or, you might found your own club and work as its executive director. Again, it will be most successful if you specialize and don't try to compete with powerful existing clubs. As you travel, you'll find your niche. Perhaps it will be to organize camping fishermen, camping BMX fans, people who own Brand X trailers, campers who square dance, or wheelchair campers.

Such clubs usually start out as a labor of love, and require good organizational skills. Still, an executive director can command (and deserve) $20,000 a year and more.

Newsletter

This will tie you down more than most of the other fields listed here, but could be the bluebird in the back yard of the fulltimer who spends all winter in one spot and all summer in another. Newsletters, which use no advertising, may be only four or five mimeographed pages yet they sell for from $12 a year to thousands of dollars depending on the demand for the information.

Again, specialization is the key. Publish a letter for snowbirds, on factory outlets, on the best antique shops, for campers who seek out wineries, for people who are looking for uncrowded campsites in Florida. Or, go outside the camping field and put your expertise to work. Publish a newsletter on investments, on black powder firearms, on fishing the Florida Keys. One woman publishes a monthly newsletter just on chocolate.

You can start with a tiny investment and hand-addressed mailings. Then, if it appears that your idea will fly, spend more to advertise, promote, print, and distribute the newletter. If it becomes so big that you can afford it, all layout, printing, and mailing can be handled for you by a fulfillment house.

Caravans

Many people are reluctant to take off alone for parts unknown, in a vehicle as complex as an RV. They need the fellowship, guidance, and security of a group. The more experience you've had in the travel industry, the better this

Figure 12. Have a work or sales table with you everywhere you travel, and your own picnic table in campgrounds where they are not provided. This compact set is from Duralite, Passaic NJ.

can work for you because your income is derived from a combination of fees paid by your members, and commissions from restaurants, attractions, and other facilities you patronize. The more attractive and unusual the package you put together, the more successful you'll be.

The Fulltimer-Writer

Because many people know that my husband and I lived on the go for ten years, supporting ourselves by writing about our adventures, we're often asked how others can make a living in this exciting, mobile, free, career field. It takes entire books and college courses to tell people how to write, what to write, and how to turn your writings into cash, but here are some highlights of what we tell others who want to travel and write about it.

First, fulltiming won't turn you into a writer. If you don't write now, you won't write on the road. Writing is not just a job but a need that bubbles up from deep inside. If you have it, you're already writing, even though you are not selling, because you can't *not* express yourself on paper. Writing is hard and lonely work, and just having the time to write or experiences to write about aren't enough to give you the discipline to stick with the typewriter day after day, week after week.

Second, writing doesn't guarantee an income. Even if you're an experienced writer now, freelancing is a new ballgame. I'd written before for newspapers, and in advertising, and was accustomed to seeing my work go directly from the typewriter to the composing room. Rejection was a new and galling experience, yet the freelance has to live with it. And even if you're a successful freelance, it takes about six months before your cash flow is enough to support your travels.

Now that the negatives are out of the way, here are some how-to's. Get a permanent address, either by using a mail forwarding service or through a relative you can trust to stick with the job day after day (see Chapter 18). Forget about agents unless you are an established writer. Agents who work with unpublished writers charge a fee, and often do little else.

Have enough of a nestegg not just to finance your full-timing, but to start a business. Like other professions, free-lance writing requires tools: a typewriter or word processor, letterheads, business cards, lots of postage, 9 X 12 envelopes, file folders, reference books, and a budget for coin-op copy machines. A camera is a definite plus for nonfiction writers.

Buy a copy of Writer's Market, a yearly reference book sold in book stores. It tells you what magazines want, and what they'll pay. It's best to deal with magazines you're familiar with, so spend a day or two in the library. Don't waste money sending poetry and fiction to magazines that don't use them.

If you have an idea for an article, send a letter to the managing editor. It should contain a summary of your proposed article, a sample of your writing style (either in the body of the letter or in the form of a copy of some published work) and a list of your qualifications for doing this writing. If the editor gives you a go-ahead, write the article and clip his letter to your manuscript when you submit it. Stamped, self-addressed envelopes go with everything you send out.

Although the beginner may have to write some articles on speculation at first, I recommend against writing for magazines which don't pay or which do not commit to assignments. If you're good enough to publish, you're good enough to be treated like a professional. I've never heard of a writer getting an assignment because an editor had seen his work in a no-pay publication. Nobody is going to pay you for doing something you've demonstrated you do for nothing.

As soon as you can qualify, (requirements vary) join a writers organization. There's a list in Writer's Market, and they range from general journalism groups to highly specialized mystery, romance, and technical writers. Such a group gives you support, market information, group hospitalization and buying privileges, and clout.

Don't count on making a living writing only about RV's, or even about general travel. You'll do best if you have a speciality that goes well with your roving lifestyle: birding, rodeos, historical architecture, fishing, hunting. Say you visit the area of Tennessee that is famous for its bald eagles, because you're a bird watcher. You can do a feature on motor-coaching in the area, another for a travel magazine, one for an outdoors magazine on the best times and places to sight the eagles, one for a pet magazine on how a volunteer nursed a sick eagle back to health, one for a children's magazine on how eagles hunt, and another for a science magazine on new methods used to protect endangered birds.

If you're a fiction writer, use your travels to add authenticity to your plots, but don't make the mistake of traveling too quickly. Immerse yourself in an area to learn all its legends, festivals, heritages, seasons, cadences. Editors have seen a hundred mysteries set in London and New York. Yours, set in a small town in Idaho, will stand out in the crowd. In non-fiction writing too, we find that the slower we travel the more stories we uncover in each area.

Keep track of all expenses connected with your writing business, then ask a tax expert how much of your motorcoach and travel expenses are deductible. The more money you make writing, the better your case. Just don't start calling yourself a writer, deducting all your travel expenses, and except the IRS to swallow it without lots of supporting documents including rejection slips and postage receipts.

Lastly, write, write, write. Even though you can choose your own hours, scenery, topics, and bosses, there is no free lunch. The more you write, the more you sell. The more you sell (or are rejected), the more you learn about the marketplace. The more you learn about marketing, the fewer rejections you'll have. Only you—not an agent, not a writing course, not a writers conference—can make fulltiming and freelance writing combine into a comfortable living.

Be a "Temp" to Fund Your Fulltiming

It's very possible that you can make money as you need it, as a friend of ours did for years, through temporary help services such as Manpower, Kelly Girl, and other such names which are found in the Yellow Pages under Employment-Contractors-Temporary Help.

For employers, the advantages are obvious. They take you or leave you, with no promises (and, frankly, hardly even a glimmer of hope) about the future. For some workers, this sort of situation would be a last, desperate measure after they have failed to get a permanent job. But for you, the full-timer who is lured back to the open road as soon as the kitty is fed, it means a job when and where you need it without promises, future, or fringe benefits. And no hard feelings when you quit and move on.

The opportunities range from auditing to X-ray technician, with most openings in the clerical and secretarial fields. Stopping at one such service, I was told that their greatest need is for a skill that many men and women already have: typing. "We have openings in light factory work, industry, and office work," I was told. And many of the temp services have their own free training programs for a skill that is in increasing demand: word processing.

"About the only jobs we don't handle are those that involve any sort of danger, because of the high insurance costs. You work for us. We pay your hourly rate, social security and insurances," said the employment counselor. Fringe benefits, however, can be skimpy so you'll be wise to fund your own IRA, hospital insurance, and other perks.

"What about the person who moves on often?" I asked. "Will you take applications from people who may want to be available for only a few weeks or months?"

"Of course!" the girl behind the desk said, surprised I had asked. "Most of our jobs last an average of two weeks. We don't mind if you move on afterwards. It's no black mark against you at all."

Even if you're fresh out of college, and have no job experience, or have been home raising children for 20 years and your experience is rusty, temp services want to talk to you. Accent the positive. In college you may have typed term papers to earn extra bucks from fellow students, worked the dorm switchboard, or cleaned chemistry lab equipment to earn meal money. Report proudly and confidently on what you've done and done well.

If you've been at home with the kids for years, list the typing you did for the cancer society, the times you managed the kitchen during church suppers, the way you organized the hospital volunteers, the telephone soliciting you did for a political candidate. If you're good with your hands there are assembly line jobs, packaging jobs, inventory. If you had experience or training, even years before, report it as a plus in your best, sell-yourself manner. Ask too if the employment service offers brush-up courses or free courses in new skills.

For those who have had extensive career experience, temping can be a letdown but look at it as a way to fund your fulltiming. You may have worked as an executive secretary before you went fulltiming, but as a temp you'll probably do routine steno work while the firm looks for someone they can groom as a secretary for the boss. You may have managed the bindery or blister packaging department before you went fulltiming, but now you'll just be another number. You may have been the top salesman with your company, but as a temp you're a door-to-door surveyor, a merchandise clerk, a product demonstrator.

By your past standards, you'll probably be dismayingly underemployed, earning less and having less authority. But remember, no matter how important you were before, you're now less desireable to the company because you want to move on. And this job is more desireable to you because you *can* move on with no ill feelings on either side.

Besides the poor prestige, either real or perceived, there are other minuses in tempting. One is that you have to be on call for short-notice jobs which could last a day or a month. This in turn means that you need good cooperation from a campground manager, who will call you to the phone, or that you'll phone the employment service frequently. They may want you to call every morning, every afternoon at 3:15, twice a day, or keep some other strict call-in schedule.

Another disadvantage is that you are paid only for those days you work, so there could be long dry spells. A more subtle debit to temping is that you'll never quite be part of the employee family, and you'll have to be extra friendly, hard working, and cooperative to overcome the "outsider" feelings both you and your fellow employees may have. You'll probably be earning less, and getting fewer fringe benefits, than the person working next to you. Still, my friend, the fulltimer who worked for years as a temp, found this wasn't a problem because other employees were fascinated by her roaming life, and they also knew she wasn't a threat to their place in the pecking order.

If you want to try temping, register with several different agencies. Find those that give you the right dollars, benefits, "vibes". When a job is offered, follow through as dependably and capably as if your entire future depended on it. A good record will follow you around the country, from one Kelly Girl or Manpower or Personnel Pool office to another.

With each job, don't be shy about asking what benefits are due you. With some services, you qualify for paid lunch hours, holidays, or health insurance after you've worked a minimum time, usually about 750 hours. The employer pays the employment service and the service pays you. *The testing and placement are free to you* and so, in many cases, are courses and testing.

One last tip. Never take off fulltiming and broke, with the expectation of finding work in the next town. Keep a cushion fund to ease you over the hard lumps in the financial road.

For more information, contact the National Association of Temporary Services, Inc., 119 S. St. Asaph St., Alexandria VA 22314. Also contact local temporary help services for helpful brochures. A book "A Guide to a Second Career" is available for $4.50 ppd. from the Business and Professional Women's Foundation, 2012 Massachusetts Ave. N.W., Washington DC 20036.

PART THREE
Go!

Chapter 16
The RV Cook

"Do you cook underway?" It's a common question, and one that astonishes me. It's foolish to travel without a seatbelt, and even more foolish to try to work in the galley underway. In a panic stop, hot foods could fly off the stove and injure someone. In hard turns, dishes slide around countertops. If there's a lurch when a drawer or cupboard door is open, everything crashes out.

The RV cook, unlike the galley cook in a boat, can always have the luxury of stopping the vehicle. That, however, is where the luxury stops. There is never enough room, enough gadgets, unlimited water, space to seat more than four or five at the table, or counter space for big projects like fussing over individual salad plates. Because of low ceilings, the coach swelters when the oven and burners are belching heat. You may not have electricity some of the time and, even if you do, there isn't room to carry all the work-saving appliances you'd like to have.

Figure 13. Sink inserts can increase counter space. Photo Credit: Terry.

Despite these obstacles, however, you're charged not just with making everyday meals but with entertaining, birthday cakes, Christmas cookies, Thanksgiving dinner, and perhaps even some canning and preserving. If money is no object, you can eat out often and make use of the fine quality and variety of convenience foods found in today's supermarkets. If you're like us, though, you can't afford restaurants or frozen meals day in and day out and besides, you prefer old-fashioned, home cookery.

Our 21-foot mini-motorhome has a full kitchen with refrigerator, freezer compartment, 3-burner stove with oven and broiler, cupboards, sink with hot and cold running water, and a couple of drawers—but all of them are sized for a dollhouse. It's a real challenge to decide what the bare minimums will be, learn to cook with them, and get used to making Texas-size meals in a Rhode Island-size galley.

As you outfit your RV, remember that you'll be on the road for many miles each year. Underway, everything must be very securely stowed so it can't come loose and be smashed (or smash someone) in an abrupt stop. At home you're used to having things within reach. The canisters and some small appliances stay on the countertop, the Mr. Coffee always has a hot cup of coffee waiting for you, the tea kettle sits on the stove, gadgets hang from the wall. In your RV everything must be bolted down or put away in locked cupboards. Even then, tall pyramids of pans or plates will fall down on rough roads and anything left hanging from a hook will sway constantly and wear a hole in the wall.

When you sold the household goods, it's probable that you kept many of your favorite kitchen tools because you use them daily. Many will continue to be indispensable aids in your new galley but many just won't be needed. Some new things you never used before will be added. Don't be a slave to habit. Never stop re-evaluating ways to make the load lighter and the job easier.

Pots and pans. Good stainless steel, nesting pans with removable handles save space, and you'll find them for sale

Figure 14. A good substitute for an electric countertop coffee maker is this thermal coffee maker from Corning. Drip coffee is made in the seraver; keeps hot for hours without electricity. Photo Credit: Corning.

at camping and marine supply stores. Among the best (and most expensive) are those from Cuisinart. Look at the Stow-away set, which costs about $500 when you add the extra lids needed.

I'm very fond of my pressure cooker, which saves time, fuel, and heat build-up in our little galley. It pays for the space it takes up because it can be used for all types of cooking plus the canning and preserving I do on a small scale when our travels lead us to a surplus of fish, berries, or other regional treats. My book *Cooking on the Go* (Hearst) tells how to bake atop the stove in the pressure cooker too.

My favorite skillet is Club Aluminum's big, Silverstone-lined chicken fryer. I use it for all roasting and frying, and use a small, open Silverstone-lined skillet for smaller saute or frying jobs. While many cooks prefer an iron skillet, I find that heavy aluminum spreads heat better on small, RV stove burners. I also carry a Nordic Ware stovetop waffle maker, an aluminum griddle that fits over two burners, and a tea kettle.

In choosing pots for your galley, consider ease of clean-up, overall weight, rust and corrosion resistance, multi-purpose uses (oven-to-table, stackable, compartmented, double boiler), size for your burners and oven, and stackability. Good choices are stainless steel with a multiple-layer bottom which spreads the heat, gourmet quality copper, aluminum, and Silverstone or Teflon coatings. Poor choices are glass and ceramics for obvious reasons, iron because it is heavy and does not distribute heat well, and porcelain-clad steel or cast iron because it chips in hard, RV use.

Dishes and glassware. I've met some galley cooks who just won't settle for plastics, so they gladly devote extra space to the bracing and cushioning needed to carry good crystal and china or stoneware. Still, the choice of unbreakables is so bright and exciting you can probably find something you like. One of my favorites is Yachting Tableware (1112 E. 7th St., Wilmington DE 19801). It comes in many patterns and colors and each piece has a nonskid ring on the bottom. This keeps the stacks much quieter in the cupboards when you hit lumpy places on the road, and cuts down on scratching and slipping. The company also makes glasses, wine glasses, non-slip paper plate holders and other clever galleyware.

Stove lighter. If your galley stove doesn't have automatic ignition, buy one of the piezo sparkers sold in camp supply stores. Matches are a menace, and messy.

Dishwashing. Only rarely are RV's equipped with dish-washers, and for good reason. They are the most space-inefficient of all appliances, they use more water than you sometimes can spare, and they save little or no time. I keep a dishpan in the cupboard under the sink and fill it as one would a dishwasher. The odd spoon, cups after a coffee break, and the occasional mixing bowl are slipped into it during the day so no dirty dishes pile up in the sink.

After a meal, I scrape dishes and stack them in this pan. Hot water and detergent are added, and everything soaks

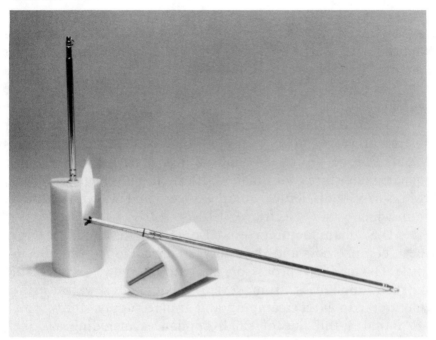

Figure 15. Various types of permanent lighters, like this Perma Match (Harper-Lee International, 308 Prince, St. Paul MN 55101) will save the RV cook the mess of matches. This type uses a butane cylinder and creates a flame, useful for lighting the oven or barbecue. Piezo-type sparkers have nothing to wear out and are ideal for lighting gas burners and the refrigerator. Photo Credit: Perma Match.

while I put away food and clean up the galley. By then it takes only a fast flick over each piece with a wad of nylon net to clean them. Rinsing under a thin stream of hot water is done in the sink, and the dishes drain in Rubbermaid's new, compact, one-piece combination drainboard and rack. If there's time before we get underway, I let things air-dry.

This system solves several dishwashing problems. It hides dirty dishes as they pile up during the day. The equipment takes much less space than a dishwasher. It's thorough. And it uses minimal water and energy.

Microwave oven. Most RV's of live-aboard size are coming out of the factories equipped with mocrowave ovens. If you opt for one of the new combination MW-convection ovens, one cavity will do the job of both a conventional, and a MW oven. The new, plastic MW cookware is sturdy and lightweight, and MW cooking is a quick, energy-efficient method that has many pluses for the fulltimer. Even if you have not been a MW convert in the past, consider how one can aid your new lifestyle.

Small appliances. Probably because of the strong dollar in recent years, we're seeing a flood of compact appliances from Europe. Look in housewares departments of large department stores for small wafflers, the all-purpose Maxim Maxi-Mix tool, Krups' folding slicer, and Maxim's Brunch Pan which is a 7" electric skillet.

U.S. manufacturers are also aware that today's cooks need compactness and versatility, so have a look at Sunbeam's little Oskar food processor and all the new, rechargeable kitchen appliances from several major housewares manufacturers. In larger camping and trailer supply stores, you'll also find a full line of small appliances including a skillet, coffee maker, toaster, and saucepan that work on both household power and 12 volts.

My favorite and most versatile electric appliance is a one-burner hot plate, sometimes also called a buffet burner. It is a full-power unit like the element in an electric stove. Instead of having many electric appliances, I can use this one burner as the thermostat-controlled element under a skillet, stovetop toaster, wok, waffle maker, percolator, kettle, pressure cooker, or corn popper. It's handy for long, slow simmering, for times when we run low on gas, or when I want to cook outdoors on the picnic table.

Now, how can you cope with mealtime? The answer will be different for each RV cook, and the adjustment will probably be more difficult for the older and more experienced cook who has a set way of doing things. Here are some suggestions:

1. *Don't make an abrupt change.* Our first weeks of fulltiming were very jarring. We'd left family and friends behind, no longer had the routine (and income) of a job, and were in new surroundings with new equipment. Homemade

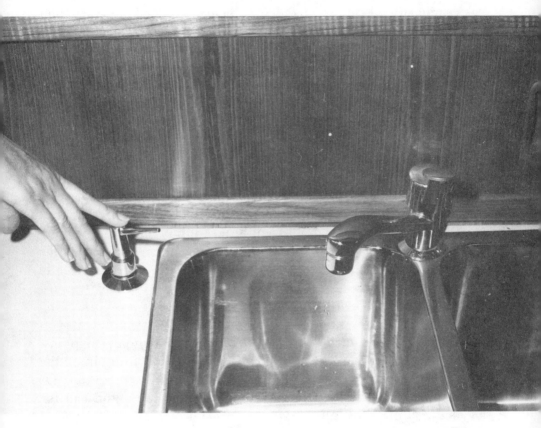

Figure 16. Install a soap dispenser (available from a commercial plumbing supplier) in the counter next to your motorhome/camper sink(s). Soap is always handy yet can't slide off underway. Photo Credit: Gordon Groene.

meals, at the usual hours, were a psychological lifeline of familiarity. For us, irregular meals grabbed at fast-food restaurants would have added to our sense of disorientation.

2. *Don't be bound at the beginning by old kitchen standards that required you to make your own bread, serve eight-course breakfasts, and use crystal goblets.* Jugglers start with three oranges, and work up to showers of apples and tennis balls. Until you get the feel of your miniature kitchen and lack of work-savers, keep menus as simple as possible. As time passes, you'll get more adroit.

3. *Find new and enjoyable substitutes.* If you loved getting out the best linens for company, and cannot manage them now, buy coordinated paper sets. If you can't wash a dozen coffee cups a day as you used to, buy an attractive mug for each family member and merely rinse them between coffee breaks. If you miss your best china, splurge for some really nice melamine.

4. *Dazzle your guests by driving them to a breathtaking view.* Let them savor it through your RV windows as you serve a simple meal on tin plates with red bandana napkins. Or give a party in the RV park clubhouse and bring in all the food, hot and ready to serve, from a Chinese take-out. Or spread a red-checked cloth on your picnic table and call for delivery of giant, all-the-way pizzas. Or think up a Dagwood Party where everyone makes his own Dagwood sandwich from platters you had the deli create for you. Or arrange with a restauranteur to reserve a table for you and your guests and serve a meal you have ordered in advance at a price you can afford. There is always a way to host friends, even those from outside the RV life who don't understand the limitations of the galley.

5. *Write a galley checklist.* Use it each time you start the RV. Make sure drawers are fully closed and in locked position, pilots off, liquids in the refrigerator securely stoppered and the door locked, and all loose galley gear snugly stowed.

Chapter 17
Managing Money on the Road

Have you tried lately to cash a check in a town where you are not known? Even at our own bank where we have been faithful depositors for years, we cannot cash a check unless we have enough money already in the account to cover it. When you're on the road as a fulltime RV liveaboard, your whole financial picture changes, no matter how rich or poor you are. In the eyes of the world, your name is Mudd.

The first hurdle is to take a fresh look at the banking world beyond your hometown. Bank charges have mushroomed in recent years, competition has heated up, and the consumer has to choose from a bewildering shell game of charges, fees, incentives, and penalties.

The schedule of rules and fees from one of our local S&L's fills two pages single-spaced. If your savings account balance falls below $250, there is a $2 monthly fee. If you write an overdraft, it costs $15. If you want to stop payment on a check, they charge $12. It costs $10 to transfer funds within the U.S. and $25 to another country. There are seven different deposit accounts, all with their own schedule of minimum deposit, minimum balance, and differing interest rates depending on the balance. In many thrift institutions, senior citizens pay different rates from those of non-retirees.

Some savings institutions offer free credit cards; other charge up to $20 a year. Some offer free travelers checks or safe deposit boxes if you maintain a certain minimum balance. Credit card finance charges, limited by state law, vary greatly from state to state. So do the rules about how finance charges can be applied.

The point is that, as long as you'll have to do much of your banking by mail anyway, it pays to keep shopping around for the best deal no matter how long you've been dealing with those friendly folks at your neighborhood bank or S&L. You could save money by having checking in one place, savings in a second, and your Visa or MasterCard account in another state altogether.

We're assuming you don't want to carry large amounts of cash. If you do, you may want to shop for a fireproof (not heat resistant and not just a metal box) safe which can be mounted in a hidden spot, in the most theft-proof manner you can devise, somewhere in the bowels of the RV. You want the box to survive not just fire or burglary, but a highway accident in which the coach is torn apart.

Here are some alternatives to cash:

Travelers checks are the solution most of us think of first. Most cost about 1% of face value, although free checks are sometimes available depending on the type of bank account you have. Even free checks, however, cost money because you're losing interest as long as you hold them. We've been in stores and even in banks that would not cash traveler's checks. Still, they are invaluable in foreign travel.

Savings bonds are the safest and most portable wealth, but be sure you understand the rules. They can't be cashed immediately after purchase so you have to plan ahead, and they can't be cashed in other countries, even in branch offices of U.S. banks. We've had bankers balk at cashing our bonds, but we learned that institutions that sell them are also required to redeem them *if* you don't ask for unreasonable amounts and if you have suitable identification. That's why we carry a passport in addition to our drivers licenses, and usually cash only one or two $100 bonds at a time.

If an institution that sells bonds refuses to redeem yours, get out a notebook and begin taking down the name and address of the institution and the name of the person you're dealing with. (It's probably on a sign on his/her desk or window). If they have been trying to bully you, this may loosen the purse strings. If they still refuse, give a full report to the Savings Bonds Division, U.S. Treasury, 1111 20th St. NW, Washington D.C. 20226.

Not only are bonds protected in case of theft or fire, they earn interest until you redeem them. Record the numbers of all your bonds, travelers checks, credit cards, and other instruments and keep them on file somewhere outside the RV.

Personal checks are simply hopeless in supermarkets and most department stores, but we use them as often as possible to keep from depleting our hard-to-replenish cash supply. Try a check first. Ours have been accepted (always) by doctors and dentists and we use them to pay all bills by mail; (almost always) for prescriptions, campgrounds, and postage charges at post offices; (sometimes) for amount-of-purchase payment in department stores, auto parts stores, tire outlets, flea markets, and other retailers and (rarely) for restaurant bills or cash in small towns.

Credit cards can be lifesavers when you're short of cash. The advantage to national credit cards and bank cards is that they can buy food, clothes, new tires, fuel, any mail order item you need in a hurry (such as a spare part), gifts in person or by telephone, and even cash.

On the minus side, some people tend to over-spend because it's so easy to "put it on the plastic". Your cards could be stolen. Credit card companies sell their mailing lists, which means tons more junk mail chasing you. And, if you don't pay the bill on time, interest rates are in the staggering, 15-20% category.

As we mentioned before, shop around for these cards. Some savings institutions offer MasterCard or Visa free. Costly, prestige cards such as American Express and Diners Club include other advantages such as a slick, monthly magazine, which may or may not be useful to you.

Oil company credit cards are usually free, but use yours carefully. Some service stations charge more for charge purchases than for cash sales. Some charge no more if you use their credit card but more if you charge on another oil company's card. In any service station, make sure you understand what is to be gained and lost by using credit.

Before you take to the open road, get a telephone credit card because it will be more difficult to get one after you no longer have a home phone. It saves the delay and awkwardness of feeding coins into a phone, or the inconvenience to others of your making collect calls.

A good credit card rule is to keep the tissue copy you get with every sale, and check your bill against this total. Most companies now no longer send you a copy of the entire bill, so it's harder to keep track of what you charged, where and when. In those rare instances when a merchant has kited the bill after you signed it, you'll catch it.

Credit card theft is an increasing problem. Claim your carbons, be very close about giving out your card number, and report any theft immediately. Keep a copy of the card number, and the phone number where you should report a theft, handy in the RV and another copy with someone at home.

Some credit card companies permit you to pay bills without enclosing a copy of the bill. Here's the scenario: you are traveling cross-country and will not get your mail for another month. Yet you keep all your carbons, know your balance, and want to pay the bill before any finance charges are added. Some companies allow this: others have no way of dealing with checks that come in without all the necessary paper work. Ask about your company's policy.

Ask your credit card company too how to use your card to get emergency cash. With many cards you can go to a bank, S&L, supermarket, or even a roadside teller, and charge cash just as if you were charging a new sweater. Interest starts immediately, not at the end of the billing period as it does with other purchases, but it is worth it if you're in a spot where you can't get cash any other way. How much cash can you get? It's different for each person, and is not necessarily based on the credit line that is printed on your statement.

When we went fulltiming, it was some months before we realized our wallets were bulging with cards we never used. We pared down the list to the major oil companies, national store chains such as Sears and Penney's, and one of the bank cards. Many big chains and department stores such as K-Mart have their own credit cards but also take bank cards. We never carry two cards, and pay two bills, where one will do.

We've been in large department stores where "instant" credit is offered. They won't accept your Visa or MasterCard, but will accept it as a credit reference in opening a new charge account in this store. So we sometimes make use of this, charge a string of purchases that same day, pay the bill when it comes and cut up the new credit card when it arrives because we'll probably never be in that city again.

If you use your credit cards regularly, and pay the bills on time, new ones will automatically arrive. Watch the dates, though. The cards may die automatically of old age if you don't use them. In any event, here's where it pays to have a good, dependable mail forwarder because many credit cards come in envelopes instructing the post office not to forward them automatically. If the mail is not delivered to your mail forwarder as the final recipient, it goes back to the credit card company and it takes months to get the machinery in motion again.

Cashiers checks Don't count on them for instant cash in towns where you are not known. We've had to wait three or four days for such checks to clear.

Other wealth Don't underrate the value of having on hand enough food and spare parts to see you through lean times. Both are cheap insurance.

Money Market Account These high-interest accounts are offered not just by banking institutions but by stock-brokers. Compare the advantages of the many different accounts available. Usually they pay top interest, have check writing privileges, and include other services such as credit card management.

Transfers Let's say you're on the road and need money right now. There are several ways to transfer funds. One is by wire. Your friend takes the cash to Western Union and tells them how to reach you. Depending on how much traffic is on the wires, this takes a matter of hours and costs about $25 to wire about $500.

Postal money orders are under $2 for up to $500, and they too can be cashed almost anywhere. Your friend or relative back home can get one to you fastest by 24-hour Express Mail or one of the delivery services such as Federal Express. If you're using Express Mail, keep in mind that there are two types: post office to post office, and home to home, and they're not available everywhere. The disadvantage of delivery services is not all of them deliver on weekends, and they go only to street addresses, not post office boxes.

Other electronic transfers can be handled for you by banks and brokerages, especially if you're a customer of a national chain.

Power of Attorney A durable power of attorney contract allows someone at home to act on your behalf in all sorts of matters. See your lawyer about how one can benefit you.

We also made good use of a poor man's "power of attorney" by opening a joint bank account with Janet's parents. This allowed Mom to deposit any checks that came in the mail during times when we were on the road and were not receiving mail (she was also our mail forwarder). She could draw on the account to pay any bills which she couldn't get to us, to reinburse herself for postage she used to forward our mail, and to do all sorts of other favors for us.

If there was a death in the family, we asked Mom to order flowers and charge our account. If there was a wedding or graduation, Mom took our share of the family group gift out of the account. When we spent a couple of weeks at their home, we made all our long distance calls from their phone at direct dial rates (which are much cheaper than credit card rates) and Mom charged it to our account when the bill came.

There are many reasons why a joint bank account is not a good idea. There can be problems about inheritance if someone dies, and there's always the problem of who pays the tax on the interest. So we kept the balance on this account low enough to avoid problems but high enough to cover routine affairs—usually no more than about $250—and it proved to be an invaluable convenience.

Financial Ways and Means

Managing your resources is more than just taking care of cash, investments, and bills. Because you live nowhere now, you can "live" many different places depending on how it will benefit you best. Here's how: hospital insurance rates vary greatly around the nation. If you pay your bill through a Kansas address, it will be far less than if your forwarding address is in New York. State RV licenses vary around the nation. (We won't list them here because they change from year to year at the whim of politicians.) By talking to others at campgrounds, compare these fees. If you can use the address of a friend or business associate in one of the best-buy states, use it.

Some state laws require that bank accounts and safe deposit boxes be frozen if one partner dies. Avoid them. Keep your stocks and other investments in a state that has no income tax, and pay your federal income tax from there. Vehicle insurance rates are much higher in some counties than in others. Use an address where rates are cheapest. Have your will in a state that has no inheritance taxes, and it could save your heirs thousands of dollars.

The one cardinal rule in all these instances is to be scrupulously honest. If you're truly a rover, fulltime on the go, that is one thing. If you really spend most of your time in one or two places, and are using a phony address just to defraud an insurance company or avoid taxes, your insurance coverage could be voided and you could be liable for stiff tax penalties. And if you continue to vote in one state and claim residence in a second, you risk running afoul of voting authorities too.

Fulltime roving by RV can be a pain in the financial seat, but it can also be used, legally and morally, to reduce your costs to rock bottom.

Chapter 18
Mail on the Trail

Whether it's a letter from Aunt Hattie, a pension check, or a charge account bill, regular and dependable mail service is important to us all. The problem when you're on the road is how to get all the mail you must have without paying to forward tons of junk mail you *don't* want.

During the ten years we lived on the go, we had not only the usual personal and business mail, but all the mail necessary to our freelance writing business too. We couldn't have managed without the help of my folks.

It's best, if you can manage it, to establish one permanent forwarding address with a relative, secretarial service, lawyer, bank, post office (this has limits), or friend. Because constancy is so important, don't use friends or relatives except in very special circumstances. To send your mail to you faithfully is drudgery, and few friends and relatives will be as meticulous as my parents were for those ten long years.

The other drawback to having friends or relatives handle your mail is that they learn a lot about your affairs. You may not want Uncle Barney to know you're getting perfumed letters from somewhere in Spain, that you're hearing from a hairpiece manufacturer, or that you're still getting dividends from that old gold mine stock.

In our case, we not only allowed the folks free access to our mail, we welcomed it. Mom sieved out checks and deposited them for us. When we were in other countries, where we had to get forwarded mail at very high airmail rates, she threw away envelopes, trimmed letters, and eliminated unnecessary poundage. In the rare instances where the mail indicated some emergency, she tracked us down on the road.

The chief advantage of having a trusted relative handle your mail is that you get completely custom service. I could tell the folks what I needed in a hurry, what magazines to send on and which to abandon, and if there was any advertising or catalogues I wanted to receive. I could ask them to hold the mail as long as necessary, then telephone and tell them to unleash it.

When we were out of reach for long periods, I could even ask Mom to intercept bills and pay them out of a joint account (see Chapter 17) so we wouldn't have to pay high interest rates. When we were in one spot for long periods, the folks filled out U.S.P.S. forms that result in automatic forwarding of first class mail. When we hit the road again, they'd have forwarding stopped so the mail would come to their house again.

None of the other mail forwarding options, except perhaps those that cost a great deal, can think for you in this way. Usually you have to elect that all newspapers and magazines come, or none. All bulk mail or none. The letter that says you have only ten days left to claim a forgotten bank account before it reverts to the state, straggles in with same stack of mail that contains a chain letter and a discount coupon from a plumber back in your home town.

Some of the camping organizations such as the Good Sam Club and the Family Motor Coach Association offer free mail forwarding. One very reliable commercial forwarder is M.C.C.A., P.O. Box 2870, Estes Park, CO 80517. They charge an annual fee, plus a small deposit to pay postage as needed. One of the advantages to this service is that they have a 24-hour telephone, (800) 525-5304. You can call any time and leave a message on the answering machine about where you are, and when and how you want mail sent to you.

Another choice, if you always winter in one place and summer in another, is to have stationary printed, listing both addresses and the dates you spend at each. For example:

John and Mary Brown

10 Locust St. Space #32	**P.O. Box 142**
Bar Harbor ME 09887	**Key West FL 33333**
May 1-September 30	**October 1-April 30**

Then hope everyone will get it straight. You'll probably have to notify all magazines, banks, and other business correspondents every six month anyway, but this letterhead will help your friends and relatives find you.

Except for the stationery shown above, I caution against trying to keep all your closest friends and relatives current on your ever-changing addresses. Although it's a constant fight to convince Aunt Maude that your mail must go to your parents in Albany even though she knows full well you're in Albuquerque, that's better than trying to notify all the Aunt Maudes in your life every time you want to move on. If you notify some and not others, there are hard feeling. Despite your best efforts, some mail arrives after you leave, because Aunt Maude got her signals crossed. Have only one address, and stick to it.

If you're going to be away for only a year, you might prefer to keep your home address. For the first year, the post office will forward mail from your old address but after that there is no more Mr. Nice Guy at any price. Everything goes back to where it came from, even if the Postmaster knows where you are.

The only way around this is to move back home for a while, or have someone accept your mail there as if you lived there. Then start the forwarding cycle all over again. The chief advantage to post office forwarding is that it's free for first class mail. (Other forwarders have to add new postage.) You can elect to have other classes abandoned or returned to senders. If you want them sent to you, put some money on deposit with the post office for forwarding and send more as it is needed.

When you're on the road, the best places to get mail are (1) c/o friends or relatives in towns you'll be visiting (2) c/o the campground and (3) General Delivery unless, of course, you'll be in one spot long enough to establish a street address or rent a post office box. Keep in mind that package services such as U.P.S. and Federal Express can't deliver to General Delivery or a postal box.

If you're sending away for something, give a street address or insist in triple underline that it come via mail (even this doesn't always work; some companies use nothing but package services.) If you're in a super hurry for a check or spare part, and have no street address, use Express Mail. It can't guarantee overnight delivery from all post offices to all addresses but you can have it come right to the post office.

When you leave each camp, leave a forwarding address behind even if you don't know where you're headed to leave your permanent forwarding address. Otherwise, undeliverable mail goes back to the sender. He sees that your everyday address, the one he has on file, didn't reach you and neither did the address the mail was forwarded to. So he thinks you're unreachable. Have your mail forwarder put a sticker with his return address over that of the original sender. When something like a Visa bill goes back stamped "Addressee Unknown" or "No Forwarding Address" your creditors get panicky.

General Delivery is not only a reliable address in most cases, it can lead to pleasant travel experiences. Choose small towns. In large cities, General Delivery goes to the big post office which is almost always downtown in the worst location to reach by RV. In smaller post offices which see little General Delivery mail, you'll be remembered. We've walked into some very small post offices where we were greeted like friends. Our mail had been piling up, and our name was familiar to them.

At small town post offices you find easy parking, more individual service, and less chance of mix-up. Our name is Groene, pronounced GRAYnee, and several times I've been told there was no mail for us even though I knew there was some. The problem was that they had looked under R for Raney or H for Haney. Now I print the name and hand it through the postal window. At many post offices, you're asked for I.D. so have it ready just in case.

Another way to make sure you get all the mail that has been forwarded to you is to instruct your forwarder to mark the packets 1 of 4, 2 of 4, and so on. That way you know you've collected all 4 packets due you.

Postal workers are permitted to hold your letters in General Delivery for only a limited time, usually 10-15 days. If you're delayed in reaching a town where you have mail waiting, put in a call to the postmaster or, better still, send a letter. By law, he's required to return all unclaimed mail within a certain time limit unless there are *written* instructons to the contrary. We often send a postcard ahead too, asking the postmaster to keep a lookout for the large amounts of mail we are expecting and telling him the date we hope to get there.

Some other tips:

1. If your mail forwarder knows where you are at the time Certified or Registered mail arrives, he should not sign for it because it will have to be re-registered or re-certified to get the same protection when it is forwarded.

2. Make sure your mail forwarder uses enough postage. If it arrives Postage Due at a campground and the campground owner refuses to take delivery, you'll have to go to the post office to collect it. This can be a nuisance when you're in a hurry or when the post office is downtown.

3. Any time you order something by mail, or have any correspondence with any commerical concern, *mark your*

address prominently as **temporary**. Otherwise you'll get on one mailing list after another.

4. Some mailers, especially credit companies who want to know where to find you, mark envelopes "Address Correction Requested". If the post office is forwarding your mail, a postal worker who doesn't know your nomad status dutifully makes out a form telling American Express or Carte Blanche that your new address is now Applejack Campground in Kentucky. Meanwhile you've moved on to Rhode Island. We've had this happen a couple of times, and it takes weeks to straighten out. The only way to protect yourself is to warn the credit company that this is likely to happen at some time, and to remind them that they should accept no address changes except from you. Even so, computers are computers and you'll have occasional schlemozzles of this sort.

5. Often it's better to arrive at a destination before deciding which address to use there (General Delivery, campground, branch of your bank). At some campgrounds, all mail goes into one bin and everyone can root through it. We have never had any mail stolen this way, but have had letters delayed for months because they ended up in this bin and were never forwarded.

6. If you're in a desperate hurry for a piece of mail, decide on the best course of action for each particular situation. U.P.S. Blue Label is rush service, but is not delivered on Saturday. Special Delivery may not find you if the campground office is not open. Express Mail provides overnight service only between certain zip codes. Too, there are two choices. Know whether your mail has been sent to your campsite or whether you're expected to pick it up at the post office. We once chewed our nails for two days, waiting for Express Mail at the campground because the sender hadn't told us it was sent to the local post office.

7. The post office forwards first class mail free to Canada and Mexico. We've had excellent mail service in Canada; in Mexico things are more casual. Relax and enjoy the manana pace. When you're asking for your mail here and in French

Canada, it's especially important to print your name in large block letters because of the language differences. In Mexico, V is pronounced like B, and they might look for Mr. Thayer's mail under S. In Quebec, you might ask for mail for CarpenTEAR, but they're looking for Car-pawn-TYAY. Any time you're outside the U.S., remember to use local postage. U.S. stamps won't work.

Chapter 19
The Mail Order Maze

Because we all receive catalogues by the ton, wanted and unwanted, let's talk about ways they can be a boon to your roving lifestyle. First, they are an easy way to send gifts without having to shop, wrap and mail. Many catalogue houses will gift wrap for an extra dollar or two. Others, most notably fancy food purveyors, specialize in taking care of your gift list for you.

Second, catalogue orders can be your quickest way to receive a piece of equipment for your coach. When you're in a strange town you have to wander from store to store, looking for what you want at the best price. Mail orders, by contrast, come right to your campsite, post office box, or General Delivery.

Third, in your ever-changing world, mail order outfitters are consistent. Instead of driving all over a strange city to find the brand of shoes you like, a jacket in your hard-to-find size, or underwear in a quality you can depend on, you can shop at the same "store" all the time, no matter where you are.

Fourth, catalogues carry the oddball items that make fulltiming more compact, more economical, and more comfortable. Living in homes that are half the size we're used to, and which lurch about, we have special needs in all kinds of homemaking equipment. I constantly outfit our coach from RV, kitchen specialty, tool, novelty, and marine catalogues.

Fifth, large catalogue stores offer you a bigger selection than you can find in most local shops. Small towns which don't have department stores may have a Sears or Penney's catalogue store where you can see all the latest sale catalogues, and place an order which will arrive at the store (which solves a problem for you if you don't have a local address).

Despite its large size and weight, we find it worthwhile to carry the big Sears catalogue with us. We order from it constantly and use it to send gifts. It's also useful as a price reference/buyer's guide. Say, for example, we're shopping for something complicated such as a VCR. By reading the catalogue we can acquaint ourselves with the terminology, features, and prices of various VCR's before talking to local salesmen.

Here are some special tips about catalogue orders when you're fulltiming:

1. On every order note, "Not a permanent address; please do not place on your mailing list. Do not delay for back orders. Fill order promptly, or send cash refund."

2. Some mail order firms simply will not use the U.S. Postal Service. Yet parcel services can't deliver to General Delivery or a post office box. Use a street address for all mail orders.

3. Emphasize the importance of orders coming to your *current* address. Packages can't be forwarded unless new postage is paid.

4. Where a check-off box is provided, indicating that you don't want your name added to this or any other mailing list, use it.

5. When you're making price comparisons between local purchases and catalogue buys, factor in postage and

sales tax. Some catalogue outfitters pay all postage; others pay a hefty portion of it; still others charge a set fee which may be far more than the actual shipping.

6. Cataloguers must charge sales tax in all states where they have outlets. Read the fine print because so much depends on where you are and where the cataloguer operates. If you are buying a very expensive, but very lightweight item (such as jewelry or a camera lens, it's often cheaper to buy it via mail order and pay the postage rather than local sales tax.

7. Deal with established catalogue houses. There are dozens of names you'll recognize. Newcomers may not cut the mustard. If you do run into a flimflam, contact the local postmaster and a city or state consumer affairs bureau.

8. Allow 4-6 weeks for your letter to arrive, for the order to be processed, and for merchandise to be shipped. Most orders come faster than this, but be prepared for the worst. If you need something much sooner, telephone your order and charge it to Visa or MasterCard. Some mail order outfits give you the option of regular mail, or super service at extra cost.

9. As you leave each campground or address, advise the people there to abandon any catalogue mail that arrives for you even if you're counting on them to forward first class mail and other personal mail such as the hometown paper. Despite your best efforts, you'll get on countless mail lists and catalogues breed like bunnies. It's best to leave forwarding instructions in writing.

10. Save every scrap of paper that comes with your mail order and enclose a photocopy of these records with any follow-up correspondence. It's difficult enough to make claims or exchanges when you live in one place. When you add a constantly-changing address to the equation, you'll blow the computer's mind.

11. When you order by credit card, keep careful records. We reveal our card number only when we're in a desperate hurry for a spare part or other need. Once, after an agreement

was made over the phone, we received a bill for far more. Fortunately, we had the original ad from which we ordered, and took the matter to consumerism authorities.

12. While none of us like to pay high forwarding charges for junk mail, most of us do enjoy catalogue shopping, browsing, dreaming, or comparison shopping. Start a catalogue exchange bin at your campground, so campers can help themselves to unwanted, leftover, duplicate, and unforwardable catalogues.

Chapter 20
The Mysteries of Mobile Medicine

The haunting fear of being sick and friendless in a strange town is always a threat, and sometimes a reality, in the lives of all of us who wander. In a lifestyle full of wonders and rewards, this is one unpleasantness which has to be planned for.

At best, you have moments of embarrassment when you're in for a check-up and the receptionist asks the usual questions: address, employer, telephone number. Most fulltimers don't have answers, at least easy answers. At worst, you could have an emergency and be turned away at the hospital or, because you're a stranger in town, get stuck with a fifth-rate physician.

In our ten years of fulltime travel, we had one hospital emergency and a number of painful, but not serious, problems such as swimmer's ear or root canal work. We also had regular physical and dental check-ups and the occasional dental emergency. The most important point is that we survived them all, no matter where we were, with a heightened sense of affection, gratitude, and respect for our countrymen.

Our one hospital episode was at Broward General in Fort Lauderdale. Even though we had no hospital insurance at the time, we were admitted at once, treated immediately, and billed later. If you do have an emergency, get on the CB and find out where the nearest emergency center is. Not all hospitals have emergency rooms, and not all hospitals are in a hurry to admit people who have no insurance. A growing trend around the nation is to non-hospital, "free-standing" emergency treatment clinics.

It's always best to have one physician and dentist if possible, not only to assure continuity of care, but because many physicians charge a premium price for the first visit. This is only fair, because of the time it takes to record your medical history, but it adds $25 or so to the cost every time you see a new doctor. We know fulltimers who plan their travels so they can have an annual check-up at the same clinic. They travel there for any non-emergency treatment too. If they have a medical emergency elsewhere, all their records are available from this one source. (Another choice is M.A.S., below).

When we started fulltiming, never to return to our family doctor, we realized we'd have to take a lot more responsibility for our own medical care. Nobody calls to remind you it's time for a check-up; nobody but you knows the names of medications you are taking, how much you weighed a year ago, what year you last had a tetanus shot, whether that mole on your ear has changed shape or size, and what your blood pressure is normally.

We asked our hometown dentist for a full set of our latest X-rays, and we carry them to this day. Even though a new dentist will want new pictures, he's often able to learn much by comparing new to old. Recently, a dentist almost jumped for joy when he learned we had some 15-year old X-rays he could study for comparisons.

We also carry World Health Organization cards, listing immunizations and their dates (ask your doctor for one; veterans also have a record of shots they received in the service), a copy of a blood profile I had done as a base-line reference for comparison with future check-ups, and an informal note-book listing sicknesses and any drugs that were prescribed. Incidentally, you may have to ask your doctor to instruct the pharmacist to label every prescription. This isn't always routine and, in some areas, pharmacists aren't permitted to label drugs unless directed to by the doctor. You need to know exactly what you are taking.

We're both in perfect health. The more complicated your medical affairs, the more you should know about your case to tell doctors you deal with in your roamings. There's no reason why the fulltime RV life can't be enjoyed by paraplegics, diabetics, and others who know how to live with physical limitations.

Before you part company with your hometown doctor, take care of any elective surgery you need and get it over with. Have a check-up, get new glasses, have your teeth cleaned and checked, and get a supply of all the medications you take. It's also a good idea to get spare eyeglasses or contact lenses.

Have the doctor help you put together a first aid kit which includes, if you'll be deep in the wilderness for long periods, things you wouldn't ordinarily keep in the house: a snake bite kit, strong pain killers, splints, elastic bandages, butterfly bandages, icebag, heating pad, and a tooth repair kit. If you'll be far from civilization, and may have to get medical advice sometimes by radio or telephone, carry instruments for checking ears, nose, blood pressure, and heart so you can relay information over the wire.

An excellent source of such aides, except for prescription medications, is Indiana Camp Supply. Write them for a free catalogue at P.O. Box 211, Hobart IN 46342. Another source is Edmund Scientific, 101 E. Gloucester Pike, Barrington NJ 08007. We also took a course in CPR, and bought a couple of good first aid books.

Wilderness Medicine (ICS Books) by William Forgey, M.D. tells you what to do until you can get someone to a doctor. The *Merck Manual* is a physician's reference but can be useful to the layman—especially if you're in the backwoods. *The Ship's Medical Chest and First Aid at Sea* is available from the Government Printing Office. It's a manual for medical officers aboard ships which do not have doctors aboard, so it covers things the layman has to deal with when no medics are available.

Don't forget such preventive items as sun screen and insect repellent, vitamin-mineral supplements if you take them, and dental supplies your dentist wants you to use faithfully.

Three lifesaving tips make special sense when you go fulltiming. Lose weight. Quit smoking. And use seat belts. Overweight, smoking and highway injuries are among our nation's leading killers; all can be corrected by you, starting today. When a mandatory seat belt law was passed in Australia, some departments of some hospitals had to be closed for lack of business. Charlie Kittrell, executive vice-president of Phillips Petroleum Company and an expert on wellness, says that a third of all highway deaths could be prevented by seat belts.

Health insurance can be very costly when you're on the go unless you're on Medicare, or can plug into a group plan. Look into all the options you can find, starting by asking around your home town before you leave. You may be able to convert the group policy you presently have at work, without taking a new physical exam. Your insurance agent may have a policy you like, or you may be able to get group coverage through a professional organization. Keep examining and comparing what you get for the money.

If you're in good health and expect to be for some years, a "disaster" policy can be an excellent buy. The higher the deductible, the lower the premium. You pay the first $1000, $2500, or $5000 of any claim, but you're covered for a really bad illness or accident at prices far below full-coverage policies.

N.E.A.R. is service that has special appeal to fulltimers who want to be taken back to a "home" hospital in an emergency. You pay $360 per person per year. If you're injured or taken ill anywhere but in your home county, and if the attending physician determines that you can't travel except by stretcher, you're transported by highway or air ambulance. Get details by phoning them at (800) 654-6700 or write them at 1900 N. MacArthur, Oklahoma City OK 73127.

Another service is Medical Advistory Systems, Box 193, Pennsylvania Avenue Extension, Owings Mills MD 20736. For a onetime fee of $45 per person, plus a yearly update fee of $20, they'll keep your medical history on file. An extensive form is filled out by your doctor, complete with all available information including EKG. If you're taken ill or are hurt on the road, this information is available to qualified medical personnel through a 24-hour, toll-free telephone number. Write MAS for full information.

Group health and Medicare supplement plans are offered through RV organizations including Family Motor Coach Association, 8291 Clough Pike, Cincinnati OH 45244 and the Good Sam Club, 29901 Agoura Rd., Agoura CA 90301. Both organizations are recommended for these benefits as well as many others. An inexpensive policy that covers you when you travel in other countries, including Canada or Mexico, is available from International Travelers Association, P.O. Box 247, Frederick MD 21701-0247.

In any event, know exactly what coverage you are getting in any policies, particularly those aimed specifically at travelers. Some offer very good death or accident benefits, but don't cover illness. Some are good only outside the U.S. Some may duplicate coverage you already have in another policy, such as the medical payments clause in your RV insurance. A policy may cover fares home but no treatment, or may offer just a list of English-speaking, member doctors in a foreign country.

Living on the go sets up certain problems in medical care, but it has its advantages too. If you need a specialist for a particular problem, just drive your entire household to the Mayo Clinic, Houston, Memphis, or Louisville and get the best expert available. The other advantage of living nowhere, is that you can live *anywhere* as far as your insurance company is concerned. Health insurance premiums vary widely around the country—very high in New York, more modest in central Florida. If you stay in one spot, don't try to cheat. But if you really live on the go, pay your premiums from an address in one of the states where policies are cheapest.

Preventive medicine, good insurance, sound nutrition, weight loss, wearing seat belts, and kicking the tobacco habit are at the core of your healthful fulltiming years. So is exercise.

Fitness and the Fulltimer

One of the biggest frustrations in fulltiming is lack of room, especially for those of us who enjoy an exercise program. Even the largest motorcoach doesn't have headroom high enough for stretching, floor space enough for the merest calisthenics and floor exercises, or storage space for bulky workout machines.

Yet, according to Phillips Petroleum president Charlie Kittrell who leads his company's involvement in fitness programs, exercise to build strength, flexibility, and endurance is the first key in a total living-well program that includes rest, nutrition, stress management, attitude, and other disciplines.

"Today 70 million Americans, or nearly half the population, exercise each day," says Kittrell. "This year alone Americans will buy 20 million pairs of running shoes and 10 million leotards, and will fork over 10 billion dollars for everything from health spa memberships to home exercise equipment."

For those fulltimers who want to get on the bandwagon, there are a number of choices. One is simply to exercise outside the coach, no matter what the weather or who is watching. Running, which some people favor, speed-walking which I prefer, and biking are workouts you can do anywhere without feeling foolish. They're part of the pleasure of camping, and enjoying as many outdoors sights, sounds, and scents as possible. Those who spend enough time in one campground can organize an exercise group to meet at a certain time each day in the clubhouse.

Many of us need the leadership and guidance of an expert in keeping to a aerobics, jazzercise, or body-building program but there are barriers when you're on the go. The most economical programs, complete with swimming pool and other equipment, are usually at YM/YWCA's but each one is independent. If you join in one city, your membership isn't recognized in the next place you set up camp. You can sign up for individual programs at non-member rates or, at some Y's, pay the discounted "guest" rate if you're a member of Y in another city.

One small-town Florida Y charges $250 a year for family membership, but 13-week programs which meet two or three hours per week are as inexpensive as $28 per person. The Y might be the best bet for you, depending on how long you linger in one spot.

Another choice is to join one of the nationwide health club chains such as European Health Spa, Holiday, or All-American. Check the Yellow Pages. Larger chains have affiliates in hundreds of cities around the United States and, with a little scheduling, you can always be within reach of one.

Explore carefully before you join, to make sure:

1. Your membership will gain you access to all the chain's membership facilities throughout the U.S. without extra cost.

2. You know exactly what contract costs are. Some health clubs have a very low weekly or monthly cost and a big dues at the end of the year. Read the fine print to learn what your total yearly price will be, and what you get for the money.

3. All member clubs have the kinds of equipment and training you want to stick with. The better franchise chains require their members to have certain facilities. This allows you to have continuity in your training, no matter where you are.

4. You understand the club's philosophy. Some are primarily diet clinics; others accent body building; still others stress aerobic dance, Yoga, or massage. Choose a club that

can best fulfill your own needs: general fitness, exercise to enhance your skill at tennis or mountain climbing, self defense, weight loss, and muscle building, or whatever.

Portable Equipment

There are few exercise machines which are practical for the fulltimer to carry. Some of the more compact ones are:

Fitness Master LT-35, telephone 800/328-8995. A combination walking, rowing action that simulates cross-country skiing, this device folds to 5 inches high and weighs 35 pounds.

A jumprope. Make your own, for less than a dollar.

Bike holder. The Sears catalogue lists a couple of models. On days when the weather doesn't invite outdoor riding, set up your bike inside the coach or clubhouse, and cover all the "miles" you like.

Waistline wheel. You've seen it on TV and in catalogues such as Sears. It's two wheels with sturdy handles, weighs only 4 pounds, and allows you to work midriff muscles anywhere you have enough room to spread out on the floor.

Athletic Shoes. Whether your exercise is aerobics, running, or jumping rope, it's important to have good support. Although these shoes are acceptable and comfortable anywhere, I have shoes which are specifically designed for aerobics and I reserve them just for that.

We know now that it isn't enough just to be active, to eat right, and enjoy golf, canoing, or SCUBA. According to Charlie Kittrell, you "don't have to be a gifted athlete to participate and enjoy exercise." No matter how small your rolling home, there's room for the healthful joy of exercise.

Finding Help

Choosing a doctor or dentist when you need one in a strange town is difficult because you're buying a pig in a poke, and so is he. You may have to feed a big stack of quarters into a pay phone before you even find a doctor who is accepting new patients, or one who will agree to see you immediately. Yet you want to avoid the emergency room because (1) this isn't really an emergency and (2) the cost would be enormous.

We usually ask first around the campground. If someone can give you a name, it's a starting point, and it helps you get an appointment if you can give the name of the person who recommended the doctor to you. There have been times, though, when I've had nothing but big-city Yellow Pages to work with. I didn't know where to start calling, and was unacquainted with the city so I had no idea whether I was calling 5 minutes or 45 minutes away—or whether the physician was in a location with unlimited parking or in a high-rise where we couldn't find parking for the RV.

Here's where honesty is the best policy. I started at the top of the list of specialists who could deal with my particular problem and said, "I'm a stranger in town." I then told them where I was, that I needed an appointment soon, and that I didn't know my way around the city.

More than once, a receptionist has made a special point to fit me in just *because* I'd been up front with her about our wandering lifestyle. Once, a kindly aide whose office was booked solid offered to call around and find an appointment for me, to save my having to continue making calls from a pay phone. We agreed that I would call her back in 30 minutes, and by then she had me signed up with a dentist who was nearby.

Some cities have dentists' or physicians referral services. Look for them in the Yellow Pages.

Free help is also available for some problems. By reading posters at supermarkets and laundromats you can often learn of a free lung X-ray, glaucoma screening, blood pressure test, or other mobile service. Counties have medical clinics for the indigent, but some of their services are available to anyone. We visited one once because it was the only place where Yellow Fever vaccine was available, when we needed the shots for a visit to Central America. While they were at it, they gave us a tetanus booster and a smallpox vaccination. Planned Parenthood can help with birth control and the American Cancer Society can tell you about any free screening services they have available.

Chapter 21
Housecleaning and Laundry

Your rolling home looks like a home, feels like a home, *is* your home. Yet you can't clean it like a house because RV construction differs from that of houses in several important ways. One reason is economic, to give you the most living space for the money. Another is that, to save weight on the road, manufacturers seek out lightweight materials. Properly cared for, these plastics and composites will last a lifetime, but they break down rapidly if abused.

Let's start with plumbing, which includes materials that can't take the harsh, lye cleaners you can use at home. Your owner's manual may have instructions for plumbing care, specific to whatever special valves, hoses, and tankage materials have gone into your coach.

Almost all RV sinks and showers are plastic or fiberglass. Fortunately these materials have become very popular in new homes too, so there's a good selection of non-abrasive cleaners available in the supermarket. Never use scouring powder on such plastics. They break the plastic's protective outer layers, kill the shine, open pores, and allow dirt to get a better grip. So you use more cleanser, open more pores, collect more dirt, and start a cycle in which your shiny new fixtures become dull and hard to keep clean in only a few weeks.

A good rule for any cleaning is to start with the mildest cleaner possible, then get tougher if necessary. Our fiberglass sink can be shined on most days with a dry towel. For more dirt and soap scum build-up, we use a mild spray cleaner. A few times we've picked up rust stains from campground water, and have used liquid rust remover. Use only as much as necessary, in the spot necessary, for as short a time as necessary, and rinse very well.

We've never had a problem with sink stoppage. If water runs slowly, check for blockages throughout the system because the trouble may not be in the sink trap. For instance, we have a reducer that allows a garden hose to be put on our grey water outlet in areas where campground operators welcome this water on nearby plants. It's here that clogs sometimes occur, and they are easily cleared just by removing the reducer and shaking out the accumulated matter.

If the sink does become stopped up, don't use lye. Use one of the new type plungers or one of the compressed air-type sink openers.

RV carpeting takes special abuse because you do so much living in such a small area. Gravel and sand get tracked in from outdoors, and there are the inevitable kitchen spills. First, see what preventive practice you can manage. Some campers cut pieces of plastic grass mat and glue it to each entry step. Some use an overturned wire or plastic milk carton carrier as a step. It allows dirt to fall through as you enter the RV and, as you break camp, it becomes a holder for all the odd items you have to corral as you pack up.

Our kitchen carpeting has suffered all sorts of spills. Once when we forget to lock the refrigerator door, a dozen eggs fell out and broke. Another time, a pan of beef stew landed

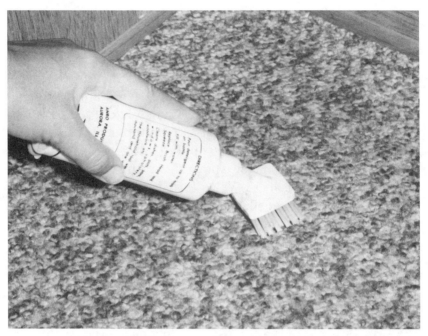

Figure 17. Soap and water dispenser sold for dishwashing use is ideal for using carpet and upholstery cleaner on small areas. Photo Credit: Gordon Groene

on the rug. Immediately, and before you start rubbing or rinsing, get as much of the spill out of the carpet as possible. Otherwise you're just diluting the stain and spreading it. Scrape up solids, then blot repeatedly with paper towels until no more moisture can be drawn up. This takes pressure, persistence, and patience.

If the spill is very wet, weight down paper towels with heavy tools or books and leave them to wick up as much moisture as possible. This not only gives cleaners a better field in which to work, it helps get moisture out of plywood underflooring before it can start a dry rot problem. After using appropriate cleaners, again use paper towels to dry the carpeting as quickly and thoroughly as possible. Blot, don't rub.

We carry a miniature vacuum cleaner aboard, with attachments, and use it very often to clean the carpeting, drapes, upholstery, screens, and other surfaces. Sears sells a dry cleaner powder called Capture which can be brushed into carpeting and upholstery, left for a few minutes to soak up dirt, then vacuumed away. We've also had good luck with some of the liquid cleaners such as Glamorene.

Starbrite, sold in marine supply stores, makes a superior waterproofer which can be sprayed on any fabrics you need to protect from splashes. We've tested it against other water-proofers and water repellents and it is the hands-down winner. Somehow, screens and fabrics seem to soil much faster in our RV than they did in the house—perhaps because so much air flows through as we drive.

The best material we've found for RV curtains is cotton. Blinds are popular, but are heavy. Fiberglass curtains, which many manufacturers use, break down from sunlight and from the abrasion caused by constant movement and swaying as the RV moves. Our heavy, embossed white cotton curtains were easy to sew, and wash and iron nicely. They allow plenty of light in during the day, even when we want to keep them closed for privacy in crowded campgrounds. Yet they are opaque enough to give complete privacy at night when the lights are on inside.

Milium lining added to window covers will darken the interior by day and add insulation against heat and cold. Newly-popular, multi-layer, insulating drapes can also be custom made by department stores and decorators.

Solar insulation films can be installed professionally or the material can be purchased by the yard for DIY instal-lation. There are various densities, depending on how dark you want to make the interior. These films add insulation and strength, but are fragile. Abrasive cleaners, or even a ring on your finger, can ruin them.

Ceilings are always a special cleaning problem. You need an effective cleaner, yet one that won't be harmful if it drops back in your face. A dripless cleaner that works

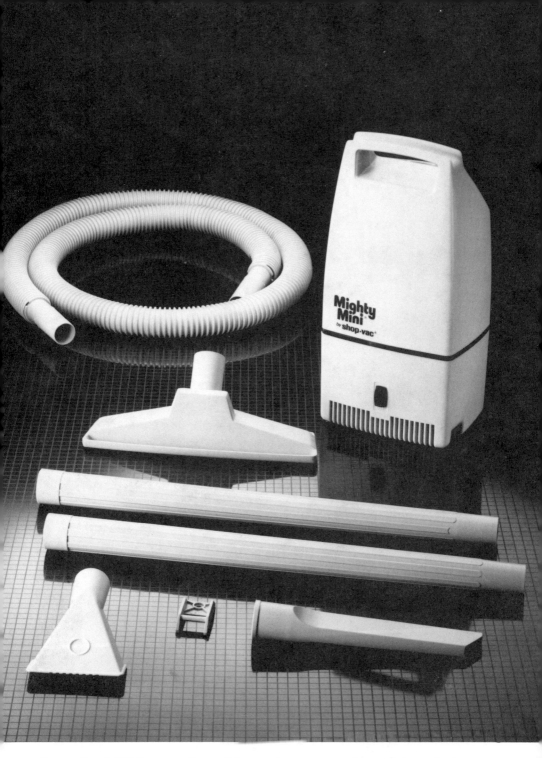

Figure 18. A full-function, but miniature-size vacuum cleaner is important to everyday RV housecleaning. Credit Shop Vac.

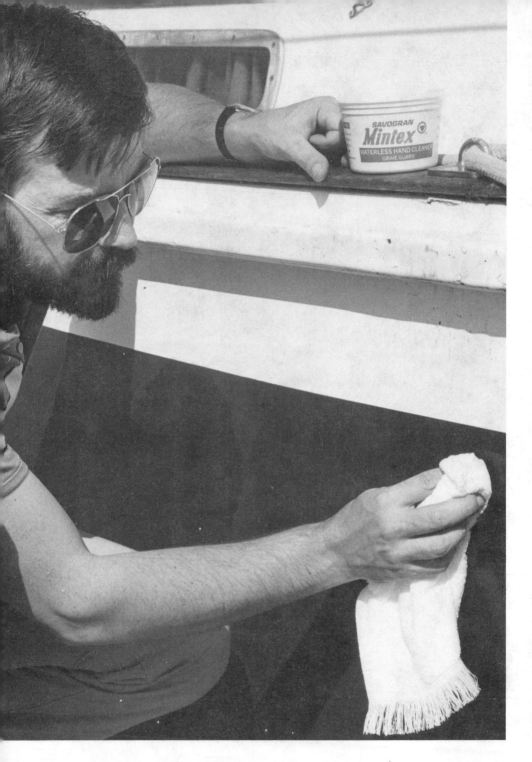

Figure 19. Waterless hand cleaners are dripless cleaners to use overhead and on vertical surfaces. Photo Credit: Savogran.

wonders for greasy build-up in the kitchen area is Goop (or try another of the waterless hand cleaners). These cleaners are extremely gentle, yet cling to the surface until they are wiped off. Wipe them in with your hands; they are formulated to work at body temperature.

Inside, as well as outside the RV, it's important to keep after rust corrosion, wear, craze, and chafe. Your house was built to last a lifetime or two. Your RV, on the other hand, incorporates materials that were probably chosen for light weight and price appeal than for your children to pass on to their children. Still, an RV can last longer if you invest extra time in cleaning, waxing, painting, derusting, and re-placing as necessary.

Washday

Some top-of-the-line trailers and motorhomes do have small washer-dryer combinations, but the results with min-iatures aren't always the best. Nor do many of us want to devote the space, water, complexity, and weight to appliances that are not needed every day.

For most of us, the answer is to use coin laundries, which are found in almost every campground, city, and hamlet. But let's go back to the first day aboard. You've equipped the RV just-so, a place for everything and everything in its place. Then you get undressed for bed that first night, look down at the socks you took off, wonder where to put them, and realize that by the end of the week you'll have to have space enough for a huge bag of dirty clothes. As you furnish the RV, don't forget some provisions for laundry.

Most RV families use laundry bags, stuffed in a locker or hung in the shower stall or on the back of a door. The more air circulation the better, so clothes don't mildew before you can wash them. We have two poplin bags each about the size of a shopping bag with sturdy, fabric handles. Colored clothes go into one; white into another.

On laundry day we grab the bags by the handles, tote them to the machine, and toss in the laundry, bags and all.

Figure 20. L.L. Bean's camper hamper holds a week's wash yet folds away into little spaces. Photo Credit: L.L. Bean.

The bags go through the wash and dry process, and are used to carry the clean, folded clothes back home again.

In our many years of travel we've encountered just about every laundry problem in the book—coin washers hooked up in reverse so you get scalding water when you want cold, washers that filled only partway or did not spin dry, machines that swallowed the money and then did nothing, dryers that burned clothes or left stains because a previous user had put in a rubber or plastic item that melted, and so on.

The moral of the story is that, although most coin machines do just what they should do, it's not wise to trust an expensive garment or your custom-made bedspread to a machine you haven't used before. One other thing. Keep a good supply of change in a special place in the RV so you don't have to go looking for dimes and quarters if the laundry is unattended.

Although we've found some coin laundries that are clean, air conditioned, and comfortable, many are hot and dirty. So we have everything ready to dump into the machines. Bleach and detergent are carried in small jars, stains are pre-treated at home with the appropriate spray, and the clothes are sorted into separate bags.

Usually, the first thing we do is to use one of our soiled towels to dust off a table so we'll have a clean place to work with the clothes when they come out of the dryer. There are never any cleaning rags around and sometimes the tables provided for folding clothes are filthy. Then we fill the machines, get them started, and leave. Come back just before they stop. Your clothes could be stolen, or dumped just anywhere by someone who is impatient to get your washer.

A few more tips on keeping clothes wrinkle-free. First, don't wad them into the laundry bag when soiled. Fold them loosely so wrinkles don't set before washing. Use a cold or cool-down rinse where available, then shake out the clothes before putting them in the dryer.

Use the dryer's cool-down cycle, or turn the heat to Low or Off for the last five minutes of drying time. Then remove

clothes at once, and smooth them firmly with your hands.
Hang or fold. Touch-up ironing is done in our RV on a folded
towel, with Black and Decker's new, folding, steam-dry,
travel iron. Some larger RV's have built-in ironing boards.
Small portables are also sold in discount stores.

If you want to do some laundry by hand, get an inflatable,
child-size swimming pool. It's big enough for large items
such as sheets yet it folds into the size of an evening purse.
A clean toilet plunger makes a good agitator for the clothes.
In John Steinbeck's *Travels with Charley*, he describes doing
his wash in a big, lidded garbage pail which sloshed and washed
as he drove the highway in his pick-up camper. (Choose a
style with a lock-on lid.) The pail serves as a hamper. When
it's half full, add water and soap and hit the road.

Wringing is very hard on clothes, so settle for longer
drying times rather than twisting the life out of them. Rig
a clothesline, or carry one of the many good drying racks
found in housewares departments. Some are free-standing,
for use indoors and out. Other styles hang up, or mount on
a bathtub.

Most fulltimers find that, of all the things they miss about
living in a house, the washer and dryer are at the top of the
list. Still, there is a bright side. No repairs. No sudden need
for $500 when an old machine dies. And, because you use
multiple machines, you can do six or 8 loads in the same time
it used to take you to do one load at home.

Mending

If sewing is one of your hobbies, you'll already have
plenty of supplies aboard. If you're an old-fashioned home-
maker, you're already listing a sewing kit that contains darning
eggs and needles and thimbles. No matter what your level
of sewing skill, however, mending is no longer a chore. It
may not even require threading a needle!

Look over notions departments with new eyes. There are
now snap-on replacement buttons, a hemming tape that
temporarily sticks a sagging hem back in place, and all kinds

of iron-on repairs including patches, iron-on pants pockets and fusing fabrics that can be used to put two other fabrics together. Singer also makes a cute little battery-operated sewing machine. Look for it at Singer centers.

Chapter 22

Maintenance: Your RV's Utility Systems

The Water System

Two types of water systems are in general use in RV's. One uses a pressurized tank and an air compressor to maintain pressure in the water pipes. The other combines an unpressurized tank with a water pump that pumps water as you need it. There are advantages to both types, so you may want to weigh them if you are in the market for a new RV, are installing a water system in a coach you are converting to RV use, or are considering a change from one type to another.

If you have a pressurized tank and will plug into campground water each night, you can travel with the tank half full, with a reserve of compressed air, so that the compressor will seldom have to run during the day's modest needs (flushing the toilet, making coffee, washing hands). The more full the tank, the more often the compressor has to run to keep adding air to the tank. The system was designed for trailers, back in the days when battery power was limited and had to be conserved.

Another advantage to this system is that the water supply is constantly changing and is kept fresh because, when you're hooked up to campground water, flow goes directly through the tank. And water flow is usually smoother and more even than with water pumps.

The disadvantage to the air pressure system is that it uses a space-wasting cylindrical tank that, because it is steel, will eventually rust. Too, it's difficult to add to such a system if you find you need more water capacity.

Advantages of the water pump system are that it uses lighter tanks, usually plastic, that are square or rectangular to make optimum use of available space. With this type, it's easier to gauge your water capacity and to add more tanks anywhere you have room to plumb them in.

The flow of water through this system may have its jerks and starts, and you'll hear the pump zzzt off and on very briefly if you draw, say, a teaspoon of water for a recipe. This is wearing both on the pump and on your ears. Many modern water systems include an accumulator, which is simply a reserve tank with a head of air that accepts a little water while the pump is running and then feeds it back as needed. This evens out the flow.

If your system doesn't have an accumulator, it's easy to add one. We find that a tall, thin one works better than a short, fat one, and we made ours out of a length of PVC pipe. A thin one aerates the water less; better commercial versions have a diaphragm to separate air and water. This chamber can be installed anywhere in the cold water system where you have room. Preferably it should be tee'd into the main line right after the pump. The larger the capacity of this tank, the more time goes by between pump runs.

External water is connected through a pipe tee with a check valve so that outside pressure can't be applied to the tanks themselves. If you do tinker with the plumbing in this type of system, allow adequate overflow venting so that plastic tanks can't be pressurized if the check valve fails. They weren't built for it. Good plastic tanks usually impart no flavor, can't rust, and should outlast pressure tanks.

Maintenance

The first step in protecting any water system is to invest in a pressure limiter valve. Find one in a camping supply, RV, or marine store, attach it to the hook-up faucet before you add your hose, and it will maintain pressure below 45 psi. This valve protects your entire water network, from hose to plumbing to water filter, from excessive pressure which in some cities runs well over 100 psi.

A quick-disconnect hose is a real labor saver; so is a water shut-off at the end of the hose. Both are inexpensive and are available in garden supply departments. Picture this scene. You're ready to move on so you turn off the water faucet and want to take the water hose off the RV. But it's still pressurized and you get showered as you unscrew it. With the valve and quick-disconnect installed, you're able to turn off the hose at the camper end, flick it off the water tank, then stick on your pressure nozzle to flush out the sewer hose without having to go near the faucet.

By installing the same disconnect fitting on your other accessories, such as the spray nozzle, you can use the items interchangeably without having to turn off the supply faucet. We also find it convenient to carry a Y fitting, for use in camp-grounds where the water faucet must be shared with another camper. Invest in a good quality water hose made especially for drinking water, so your water will stay cool and taste-free. The type that folds flat saves space too.

No matter what type system you have, routine maintenance is basically the same. Tanks should be drained and cleaned about once a year, using a suitable product for the purpose. Camping and marine supply stores carry many chemicals made for water tanks' various needs. Baking soda is a safe and effective cleaner and deodorizer. Dissolve a cupful or so in a quart of water, add it to the tank, drive around the block to slosh it around the tank, then immediately flush it through the system with plenty of fresh water.

Cold weather storage is a special problem because even a few drops of water left in the pipes will freeze, swell, and

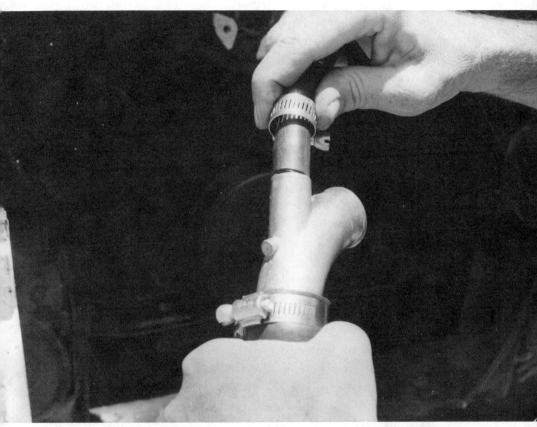

Figure 21. Hose clamps should be checked at least once a year for signs of loosening, rust, or damage to hoses. Photo Credit: Gordon Groene.

cause pipes, fittings, or tanks to burst. It's important to winterize the system according to RV manufacturer directions. Systems and instructions vary from model to model, but the aim is to drain every last drop from the system.

If you have an air pressure system, and suspect that the manufacturer hasn't supplied you with enough drain plugs to get water out of all the low spots in the system, empty the tank of water and pump up a tankful of air (or go to a gas station and use the air hose to fill your tank; run a tankful of air through each faucet which really dries out the pipes). Open the faucets and allow this air pressure to force through the remaining water.

If you have a water pump system, buy one of the commercial drinking water anti-freeze products sold by camping suppliers. Don't skimp, don't use radiator antifreeze (which can poison you) and don't use vodka (it can corrode copper pipe).

Despite your best efforts, you may end up with a split pipe after a freeze, in some spot where water collected. One of the easiest repairs for such splits is to cut it out and put in a flare tee fiting, with one of the arms of the tee pointing down, through the floor if necessary. Then put a valve on this end. The freeze occured here in the first place because this section of pipe did not drain. In the future, use the valve to drain it here each time you need freeze protection.

About once a year, check every nut in the water pressure system to make sure vibration hasn't loosened one enough to allow a slow water leak, which will drip into the RV's structure and cause dryrot. Air pumps require regular use of a special graphite grease supplied by the manufacturer to lubricate the piston. Be careful not to over-lubricate. Too much grease can get into the water; not enough allows the pump to wear. Ours gets about a drop a month.

Maintaining water pumps is equally simple. Follow directions in the manual, or on the pump itself, for oiling the bearings. A few drops regularly are better than a lot of oil once a year.

If you've ever seen the scale and debris that built up inside your tea kettle, you have an idea of what's going on inside your hot water tank. It's easy to flush it out about once a month, and without losing a whole tank of water. The first thing in the morning, after the RV has been still for some hours, let out several quarts through the drain faucet. That's enough to carry away any rust and scale that have settled on the bottom. If you install a short length of garden hose to the tank's drain faucet, water will go overboard without wetting the burner and controls.

There's one more preventive maintenance step you should take in an air pressure system that has a steel tank and copper plumbing. In time, galvanic action between these metals will weaken the steel tank. Install a short length of PVC pipe between the tank and the pipe so the two metals don't touch. Or, if you have a separate fitting supplied for the purpose, a sacrificial anode can be used. While you're installing the plastic pipe, put in a gate valve in the water outlet. This will allow you to shut off the water system in the RV, to change a washer or do other maintenance, without letting pressure off the tank.

During your RV travels you'll be drinking water from many different wells, pipes, reservoirs, and cisterns. One way to insure safety and uniformity is to add one of the many, good filtering systems that are available through plumbing supply stores, hardwares, or Sears. For the best protection, you need one that has a large filter element and which filters only the water used for drinking. (This type requires installation of a separate faucet.) Cheap, faucet-mounted filters do a less-thorough filtering job and, if you filter all water instead of just what you need for drinking and cooking, the cartridges have to be replaced very often.

Toilet and Sewer

The three types of toilets most common to RV's are 1) those that use fresh water and flush into a holding tank, 2) the recirculating toilet with holding tank, and 3) portable toilets with removable holding tanks. The first type is probably the one you'll have on a large, liveaboard RV. It's the cleanest, most carefree and most like toilets found in homes.

No matter what type you have, it probably has some sort of holding tank so some basic rules are in order:

Driving motion keeps wastes stirred up and in solution, so it's best to empty this tank immediately on reaching your campsite. Occasionally, start out with a clean tank filled about one-third full of water. Add a little detergent, and drive on. This will help soak and swish out any solids that have settled and stuck to the bottom. Again, drain immediately after you reach the next campsite.

We have never found it necessary to buy the special toilet papers sold in camping stores, or any of the chemicals. If you have a fresh water flush system and a persistent odor problem, the cause is probably inadequate venting. Adding chemicals to the tank won't help. The most common cause of intermittent stink is a piece of paper, or other solid, caught in the toilet valve, preventing it from closing completely.

With a recirculating toilet, chemicals are called for. Be sure to buy types which are safe for septic systems, which is what most country campgrounds have at their dump stations.

Most new RV's have some provision for flushing out the tank after emptying it. Ours did not come equipped with one, so one was added easily, with a few dollars worth of plastic plumbing fittings. Lucky, the holding tank vent is in a closet and was easy to reach. This was tee'd into and an opening made halfway up the outside of the camper. At the dump station, a hose can be placed in this opening to send water into the tank and out the sewer hose. Even if this water is not potable, which most dump station water is not, it doesn't matter because none of this flow can mingle with our drinking water supply.

Even if you are in the same campsite all season, don't leave your sewer drain open. Be very generous with flush water, because sewage needs extra help when you are stationary and cannot dislodge it with road motion. Empty the holding tank every day or two, flush the hose by running water through the head, then close the valve again so sewer odors can't back up into your bathroom.

If there is any sign of seepage in the sewage release valve, cure it at once because it's just plain irresponsible to let this effluent dribble on roads and campsites. Usually the cause is a tiny bit of paper or other waste caught in the seal. With the tank empty and the drain hose off, you can usually flush it clean with a garden hose and nozzle.

If the seepage continues, it probably means the valve has died and should be replaced. We always carry a spare. As you drive, try to stay aware of where the holding tank is in your RV in relation to road obstacles that might damage the tank or fittings. Be sure to protect this tank from freezing when you winterize. Don't dump greasy water into the toilet. The blackwater tank should be reserved for sewage, with all other waste going into a separate tank.

Your RV toilet should be cleaned with gentle cleaners, never with household lye products which can destory delicate plumbing parts. We regularly use Johnson's J-Wax on our plastic toilet. It cleans, shines, and protects.

Refrigeration

Most RV's use absorbtion-type refrigerators. They're unlike household units in that they have no compressors. Although these units are quiet and are usually made to work from two or three energy sources (battery power, household current, gas), they have a couple of idiosyncracies. One is that they must be either level, or in motion, or the cooling action stops. The other is that they are not as efficient and quick to recover as household types, and can usually be brought down only to about 40-50 degrees below ambient temperature. This means that on 95-degree days, your food may be kept at 50 or 55 degrees — well above the 45-degree safety level. The ammonia system used in this system is difficult to work on and should never be opened for attempted repairs.

One common failure of these refrigerators is that they sometimes won't cool down after a period of storage. If you know that the flame or heating element is working, and it still won't cool, it probably means blockage in the refrigerant circulation. Try driving over a bumpy road. If this doesn't work, remove the refrigerator from the RV and let it stand upside down for a day or two, and normal operation probably will be restored.

The gas burner, if you have one, should be kept clean and the chimney cleared of any accumulated soot. Cleaning won't be a problem if the flame is adjusted correctly. Another problem, surprisingly common, is that spiders seem to like the gas smell and may take up residence in the chimney when the RV is in storage or the refrigerator is operated on electricity for long periods. If yours won't work on gas, take off the flame windshield and look up the chimney with mirrors to make sure it's clear of spiders and webs. You may not need a repairman after all.

Air Conditioning

Some things are different about maintaining an RV air conditioner compared to a household unit. One is that inside filters need cleaning more often because you do so much living in such a small space that dust builds up faster. Outside, take off the cover on top of the RV once a year to clean out leaves and debris that collect there. Touch paint metal parts that have started to rust, clean bugs off the leading edges, and oil the blower motors if necessary. Then check the general tightness of the mounting brackets, which may start to loosen from road vibration.

Some campgrounds don't have wiring heavy enough to run air conditioning. Others are so overloaded during peak holiday weekends that voltage drops. If you hear your RV air conditioner laboring, you're placing undue strain on it and that can lead to burn-out. If you can't run the air conditioner with adequate voltage, do without it.

Propane System

This ready, efficient, cheap, easily available fuel provides you with cooking, baking, heat, hot water, and perhaps refrigeration and a barbecue without the noise and stink of a generator. With the right care, this fuel can be as safe as any other. If you ever have an opportunity to attend one of Hal and Penny Gaynor's Trailer Safety Clinics, held at campgrounds and rallies around the country, do so. Their expertise in propane safety as well as other safety concerns, is invaluable.

The gas pipes in your house can be forgotten for years because your house doesn't move. But because your RV vibrates, bounces, and twists, it's a good idea to check gas connections periodically to make sure they remain tight and leak-free. At least once a year, inspect propane plumbing with a soapy solution on the fittings. And anytime you're working around the RV, keep an eye out for any spot where gas plumbing could work or chafe from road damage or by rubbing against RV members.

Don't allow rust to build up on propane cylinders. A wire brushing and a coat of silver paint once a year will maintain them. They don't deteriorate from the inside out. Keep empty bottles tightly closed so air and dampness can't get inside. If there is a chance that air did get in, purge the bottle with a little gas before recharging it. Make sure propane bottles are well secured in the vehicle so they can't move and damage nearby pipes.

Light and Wiring

Most RV's are wired for both 12 volts and 115 volts. Our lights, television, stove exhaust, and stereo work only on battery power. (Some trailers also have one or two propane lights.) A charger automatically replenishes batteries when we are plugged into campground power, but we like using 12-volt power for television and lights because they continue to work during power outages. The household power plugs are available for use when you're plugged in, or are running a generator, for the vacuum cleaner, microwave oven, toaster, and all the other electrical aids one uses.

To make sure you never run down the start battery by over-use of lights or a radio, it's best to have two separate

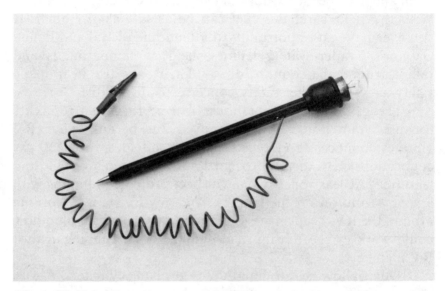

Figure 22. You can make your own 12V test light. This one is made from a ball point pen, a distributor cap seal, 12V bulb, and a sharpened nail. Use it to find 12V wiring problems. Photo Credit: Gordon Groene.

systems—one for the start battery and a second for all the "house" usages.

An inverter is a device that converts 12-volt juice to household current, and will be a handy addition for you if you have no generator but still want occasionally to use a hair clipper, electric typewriter, hand mixer, or electric drill. Just don't try to pull more power than yours is rated for. They're best for low-draw items. They're not the most economical way to use your electrical reserves, but are a quick, quiet way to create AC power when you need it for short periods.

A 12-volt test light is handy for finding failures in the 12-volt system. To check whether you're getting current at a given point, touch the probes to hot wire and ground. If there is no current, keep working toward the battery until you find the open wire or blown fuse. A multimeter will tell you how much current you have or do not have at any given point.

Exterior running lights are required by law on large vehicles like your RV, so check yours periodically to make sure they all light. Check for rust, loose or missing lenses, burned-out bulbs, bad grounds. Keep lenses clean and sockets bright.

Exterior

Your RV is a large financial investment, and an emotional investment too because this is your home. You might let a car rust away in a few years, trade it, and forget it, but your RV deserves the best care you can give it.

No matter whether its skin is fiberglass, steel, or aluminum, sun is your RV's big enemy, second only to road damage. Underneath, rust is a formidable destroyer. Keep your RV in the shade when possible and stay away from salt. If your travels take you through salted roads in winter, ask truckers on the CB where you can find a car wash large enough for your RV and give it a run-through. We avoid oceanfront campsites. On a really raucous day, there's a high salt content in winds that come off the sea. Just ask people who have to wash the windows of oceanfront homes, or look at aluminum window frames that have been battered by sea breezes for a year or two.

We keep our exterior protected with wax, and re-wax at the first sign of dullness. Johnson's J-Wax is really good for fiberglass, aluminum or steel although your manufacturer may have other suggestions depending on the formulation of the finish on your particular RV. For steel underpinnings, our choice is Texaco Compound L. Brushed on, it is self-healing. It can also be mixed with oil, and floated into areas you can't reach with a brush.

Another trouble spot on your RV is the hollow bumper or any other compartment where you store wet hoses. Touch up rust spots on bumpers and steps as necessary.

Annual roof coating is needed for some trailers and motorhomes. If your owner's manual doesn't cover this subject, check with the dealer. Even a slight leak in the roof will start serious dry rot or staining problems.

Chapter 23

Maintenance: Your RV's Engine and Drive Train

The Engine

Probably the most expensive single item in your rolling home is the engine. Whether the engine is in the tow car, pickup, or motorhome, you want to protect this investment and provide the utmost dependability. A breakdown on the road, besides being troublesome, will be extraordinarily expensive in an RV because towing charges are high *and* you may have to pay lodging bills as your RV becomes uninhabitable. It's more convenient, and more economical, to prevent breakdowns from happening.

Your most important aids are your driver's manual, any workshop manuals you can get from the chassis manufacturer, and perhaps other manuals such as those published by Clymer or Chilton for your make of power plant. The more oddball your vehicle is, the more important these manuals become because, even if you cannot do your own work, a professional mechanic may need them for reference.

Most breakdowns forecast their approach loud and clear, if only you know what to look and listen for. Then head off the posse at the pass. Take, for instance, the cooling system. Most failures here give ample warning: rusted and weakening hose clamps, deteriorated or soft hoses, slight leakage at connections, unusual noise, weepage around the water pump. All these signs point to future problems. Make replacements at your leisure, when you have the time, a place to work, and the option of picking up replacement parts cheaply at discount stores. If you don't, you could pay the piper on the road, not just with a breakdown and delays but by losing all your coolant and paying for a tow. All this because an inexpensive hose wasn't replaced in time.

Modern pressurized cooling system with overflow tanks should lose little, if any, water for as long as a year. Water in the coolant mixture can't boil away because it condenses in the overflow. So if there is any change in the amount of loss, you have advance warning that problems are brewing—problems that won't heal by themselves.

Perhaps all you have to do is tighten hose clamps, which is a good thing to do once a year anyway, to stop this loss. If you can't see any leaks, try observing all connections with the engine just started from cold, because this is when leaks usually occur. While pressure is starting to build, and before various parts expand from heat, you may be able to spot where you're losing coolant.

Any sign of air bubbles in your overflow tank is an indication of head gasket leakage. Before any permanent-type antifreeze reaches the crankcase, this trouble must be found and fixed.

Spares for your cooling system should include at least one complete set of radiator hoses and a spare water pump if you'll be in areas where you can't buy one locally. Heater hoses and any other straight pieces of hose can usually be found anywhere, and need not be carried. Also carry a complete set of fan belts. Even if you can't change them yourself, you'll always have the proper size with you.

Be faithful about changing permanent antifreeze at least every second year, because rust and corrosion inhibitors wear out in time. Usually by then the system can use a good flush

Figure 23. Check fan belts often for wear or breaks. It's important to have fan belts in every size with you to use on your RV. It may be hard to find the right size after a highway breakdown.

anyway, to wash away any abrasive particles that have broken loose.

With the engine cold, open all drains (there are usually several on the block and one on the bottom of the radiator). While the old coolant is draining, remove, and clean the overflow tank if there is any sign of sludge or scale. Then stick the hose into the radiator opening and let the water flow through freely for a few minutes. Now, with the flow adjusted so it just keeps the system full, start the engine and let it idle for ten minutes while fresh water flows through it.

Watch to make sure water flow continues to be adequate. Finally, turn off the engine, turn off the water, drain thoroughly, and let the engine cool down. You don't want to put fresh, cold coolant into a hot engine. Then close all drains, pour in the coolant, and top off with water according to directions on the coolant bottle. If local water has a high mineral or chlorine content, consider using distilled water to cut down on sediment and corrosion in the future.

Oil, like coolant, is a critical protector for your expensive engine. Many manufacturers now specify long periods between oil changes—perhaps as long as 6,000 miles—which is probably adequate if the vehicle is used continuously. When you drive long periods at a time, this keeps oil clean by cooking out inpurities and condensation. But if your RV is used for short hauls and stands idle a lot, consider changing the oil and filter more often than the manufacturer calls for. This is especially important on turbocharged equipment because turbocharger bearings are very sensitive to any contaminants in the oil.

Because most RV's won't fit on the average gas station lift, and you need a special garage for service, consider doing your own oil changes. The savings are triple. First, you buy the oil at a discount store instead of at the garage. Filters too are bought at discount stores, and you save time by working at your convenience rather than waiting in line at a garage. And, you may save on clean-up too because, if oil must be added inside your motorhome's cab, you'll be more careful than a stranger would be.

Plan to change oil at the end of a long day's drive, while the oil is hot and contaminants are in suspension. Starting the engine just to warm up the oil enough to drain well, is not nearly as good. Even an hour after a long day's drive is not too late. In fact, it's better to let the engine cool down a little to avoid burning yourself when you remove the drain plug.

What to do with the oil to avoid losing your Good Conduct Pin? Ask the campground operator. He may need it to oil an upaved road, or want it for some other useful purpose. If not, he can tell you where it can be disposed of responsibly.

Save plastic milk bottles, bleach bottles, or a cardboard box lined with a heavy plastic bag to catch the used oil.

While the oil drains, change the filter if it's also time for that. If the filter is in a hard-to-reach place, invest in a good strap-type wrench. You'll save enough by buying filters in discount stores, rather than at service stations, to pay for the wrench time and again.

After the oil has drained, replace the drain plug and refill the system with oil. Now start the still-warm engine to get the new oil circulating, especially if you have changed the filter. If you wait until the next morning when everything is cold, oil won't start circulating as readily. A minute or two of running now will be far better for your engine.

Whatever oil you choose, try to use the same brand consistently. When you're a fulltime rover, it's best to start with a brand that is sold nationwide, such as Quaker State, or internationally such as Shell which you can also get in Canada and Mexico.

Gear oil and automatic transmission oil are also available now in most discount stores. So while you're at it, you may as well start changing these oils yourself too. Your driver's manual will tell you what grade to buy.

Engine Gauges

Although the trend today is toward "idiot lights" for engine temperature and other indications of trouble, engine instruments can help keep you current on what's going on inside your engine. The vogue in top-of-the-line, Class A motorhomes is to panels that look like airplane cockpits, with all the bells and whistles. Any gauge that keeps tabs on what's going on inside your engine, generator, or other innards, is money well spent.

The following gauges, in order of importance, can all contribute to your knowledge of your engine's workings and needs:

Coolant Temperature Gauge. A light can tell you only when coolant overheats. A gauge, on the other hand, shows any rise above normal as well as too-cool operation (which means thermostat failure).

Oil Pressure Gauge. Because oil pressure drops rapidly at elevated temperatures, this gauge warns you to slow down any time you get a warning that is lower than normal.

Battery Condition. Even if you have a stock ammeter, a battery voltage gauge will tell you more about the general condition of your electrical system and voltage regulator. This information is especially important if you're using a lot of battery power when parked.

Wheels, Bearings, Brakes, Tires

Two of the wheels that were original equipment on our RV cracked within 500 miles of each other, when our camper had only 30,000 miles on it. Both times it was pure luck that we were able to stop safely, and without damage to our expensive Michelin tires.

In each case, the wheels cracked radially from metal fatigue. The point is that, once you have a wheel failure (assuming that there is not some obvious cause), suspect all the other wheels and replace them all at the mileage where the first one failed.

This rule can apply to many other parts as well, parts that were not heavy enough, or of the right material, in the first place. In the past year alone, we've seen a rash of failures in equalizer links which failed as early as 6000 miles because too light a version had been supplied by manufacturers. There have also been a lot of recent failures in imported components because of poor quality control in some overseas foundries.

Future failures will probably follow the intitial one, so get a stronger version of it or change it more often. Every time our wheels are off for painting or maintenance, they are wire-brushed and carefully inspected for signs of failure, especially around the welds. And we buy new ones every 30,000 miles.

Tire maintenance includes also providing the right pressure. If your tires tend to lose, say, five pounds a month, check them once a month and add an extra five or six pounds so they never run below the correct pressure. If you find tread wearing around the edges, you're under-inflating. Watch for signs of cupping, which usually means tires are out of balance or shock absorbers are wearing out.

Uneven wear on the front tires indicates misalignment. Because the tires used on Class A motorhomes are so expensive, you'll save greatly by spotting this wear early and correcting it at the source.

The biggest cause of damage to tires that are not on the road a lot is the sun's heat and rays. When in camp, try to devise ways to keep tires shaded. Some RV owners even have special awnings made for the purpose. A good tire paint will also help stop surface checking.

It's very important to have a spare tire—one in each size if yours are not all alike. If tires match, rotate them once in a while to keep wear the same on all of them. Just as it's important to keep your working tires out of the sun, the spare should be covered at all times. Plastic covers don't last more than a year or two. We had a sturdier one made from waterproof canvas, sewn with heavy Dacron (not cotton) thread.

Greasing the RV

Hardly any vehicles today have grease fittings. If yours does, pat yourself on the back because if you use them, you'll have lower maintenance costs over the long run than with so-called "permanently" packed joints. Your owner's manual should tell you where these fittings are and how often they should be greased.

One exception is that of a popular coach manufacturer whose owners' manual neglects to mention that inner drive axle bearings must be lubed every 24,000 miles. When failures occured, the resulting mayhem to surrounding parts has cost some owners $4000 or so. About the only way to protect yourself from this type of disaster is a) to know your RV and its needs as thoroughly as possible and b) keep talking to owners of similar rigs, and reading RV magazines, for reports of manufacturer missteps like this one.

The only equipment needed is a grease gun, preferably the cartridge type, and grease cartridges. Use a good high-pressure, lithium-type grease that can be used for all chassis fittings and universal joints.

In greasing, there are two precautions. First, any suspension parts that carry the weight of the vehicle should be unloaded before greasing if possible. (This doesn't include tie-rods.) Second, universal joints should be filled very slowly so that seals aren't forced out.

Every proper grease job includes putting a drop of oil on all hinges (gas door, entrance door, carburetor linkage, emergency brake linkage) and other fittings, to keep them free and quiet.

Brakes

Unless you have a complete set of tools and equipment for brake work, overhaul work is best left to a specialist. What you *can* do is to check the hydraulic fluid reservoirs regularly, inspect brake hoses for signs of deterioration and cuts, and keep tabs on the thickness of the lining. If your brakes are not self-adjusting, adjustment is covered in your owner's manual. Anytime brake drums are removed, be sure to clean all the dust and rust out of them to ensure smoother operation. (This debris is mostly asbestos, so don't breathe or handle it.) And always take care that no oily substances get near brake linings.

Bearings

Wheel bearings need regular service. This is an easy, straightforward job (on non-drive wheels) requiring only a few tools, the proper size cotter pins and, in most cases, new dust seals. Drive wheels get more complicated, so have a manual before opening them. Since you're saving so handsomely by doing the job yourself, spend a little extra to get the best lubricant available. Lubriplate makes an excellent waterproof wheel bearing grease.

It's especially important to keep close tabs on trailer wheel bearings, because often they aren't the best quality and they may wear rapidly. If bearings themselves show any sign of wearing or scoring, replace them with one of the better brands such as Timken or Federal-Mogul.

To adjust anytype of wheel bearing that uses a cotter pin the best procedure is to tighten the nut by hand until all play is gone and the wheel rotates freely. Then back the nut up to the next hole. On infinitely adjustable axle nuts, tighten down snugly and then back off just until the wheel rotates freely with no discernible play in the bearings.

When you prepare to repack bearings, first clean them thoroughly and give them a final rinse in clear kerosene or diesel fuel. Never dry a bearing by rotating it with compressed air, which could magnetize it. Bearings can best be packed by hand. Just put a glob of grease in the palm of one hand. By scraping with the edge of the bearing cage, you force grease up between the rollers until the bearing is completely full. This is usually all the grease that is needed unless the manufacturer calls for a specific amount in the hub.

You'll have to replace dust seals when you've packed inside bearings, so be sure the new seals are seated squarely in their grooves, with the lip facing the bearing.

One more point. Never replace just part of the bearing. Drive out the old outer race and put a new one in.

As you finish the job, be sure the dust cap fits snugly. A wheel should never be operated with a missing dust cap because even the slightest bit of grit on a roller bearing can cause failure. In a pinch, a temporary cap can always be made out of a tin can. Keep a special eye too on boots on constant velocity joints. These joints are very expensive and can quickly be ruined by a little dirt or water.

For the want of a shoe, a horse was lost. For the want of a horse, the battle was lost. Your battle against highway breakdown, equipment failure, and accelerated wear begins with preventive maintenance.

Chapter 24
Tools for the Fulltimer

The RV vacationer can wait until he gets home to his workshop, floor jack, and big toolbox to do routine maintenance and all but emergency repairs. The fulltimer, by contrast, has to deal with maintenance day by day with tools which can be carried, hired, or borrowed.

Even if you're a savvy mechanic and able to do all your own repairs you simply can't carry all the tools you'd like to have. You have to choose wisely because tools are bulky, heavy, and cost you fuel dollars every time you accelerate or brake. If you are a radish-brain when it comes to mechanical things, you need tools too because your rig probably requires some tools which a mechanic is not likely to have. How can you have tools that are both right and light?

First, we made up a basic kit, in a fishing tackle box, of those tools which are needed for almost every job. In it there is an 8″ crescent wrench, blade and Phillips screwdrivers (don't forget drivers to fit clinch-head screws and any odd screws in your coach), and feeler gauges. In this kit you'll

Figure 24. These few basic tools can do many jobs and are chosen for their versatility. With these, almost all your cutting and wrenching needs are met. Photo Credit: Gordon Groene.

need some sort of pliers, and we prefer Channel Loks because they serve as both pliers and pipe wrench. Add a side cutter, needle-nose pliers, small brad hammer, various punches and nail sets, 3 grades of rat-tail files, a couple of bastard files, and the smaller sizes from your open end/box wrench set. This basic kit weighs less than 10 pounds and carriers easily around the RV for every job from tightening battery cables to fixing door locks.

While it would be nice to have additional tools to fix everything up to such disasters as broken spring or burned engine bearings, it usually isn't practical. So let's start with more everyday needs.

Plumbing. For plastic plumbing you'll need a hacksaw, file or sharp knife for deburring, a can of PVC cement, and something that will grasp threaded PVC fittings (the Channel Loks, for instance). A short-handled plumber's helper is light to carry, and effective. For copper gas and water plumbing, carry a tubing cutter, flaring tool, and a selection of brass connectors in sizes used in your plumbing.

Carpentry. If you'll be doing any remodeling you'll need more than these tools, but for basic repairs and replacement jobs carry a hacksaw which is the lightest and most versatile saw. If you want something faster, add a keyhole saw or a saber saw. An electric or eggbeater hand drill with a selection of bits up to 1/4" will be useful. So will an adjustable hole saw. Smoothing equipment includes a plane,

Figure 25. Portable pumps or siphons can come in handy if you ever have to fuel, de-fuel, or fill water tanks under primitive conditions. Don't use any pump or line that has been used for fuel, sewage, or grey water for drinking water. Photo Credit: Gordon Groene.

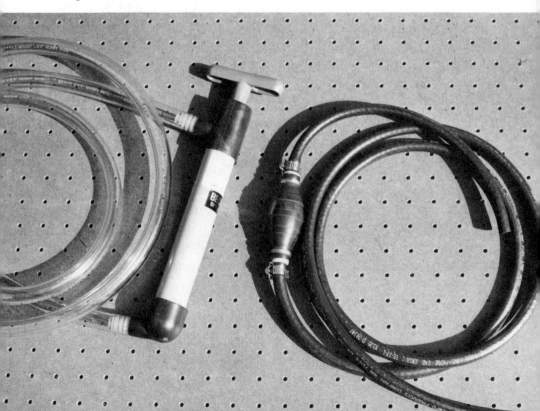

files, and sandpaper. A pint of two-part epoxy glue can mend almost anything. We carry a couple of stamped metal, spring-loaded, clothes-pin type clamps because they weigh little and exert a steady force which is good for glue jobs. You can also jury-rig clamps from rope, fishing line, or nails.

Sewing. Don't forget heavy duty thread and needles, including an upholstery needle, for first aid to cushion covers and curtains.

Electrical. Take a wire cutter-stripper, crimping tool and crimp terminals and connectors, and test equipment such as a 12-V test light or, better still, a multimeter. A pencil-type soldering iron weighs only a few ounces and is handy for small electrical repairs.

Engine and Drive Train. First, read through all manuals that came with your RV to see if any special tools are recommended. Almost every rig needs something oddball such as a special wrench to remove wheel hubs, a certain wrench to remove the engine drive pulley for a seal change, or a unique tool to remove an injector from a diesel engine. Even if you don't know how to use such tools, you should have them aboard because your hired mechanic probably won't have them. A nut splitter is nice for exhaust work, and we also carry a pulley puller because it's so handy on our coach.

In that tackle box you already have tune-up and belt-changing tools except for a prybar to get the belt(s) tight. Too, most newer vehicles require a special tool for adjusting points/ignition timing. For oil changes, add a tool to get the old oil filter off. Somewhere you should also have the larger half of that open end/box wrench set (up to 1″), larger screwdrivers in types and sizes suitable to your coach (they double as prybars), and a spark plug wrench and/or injector tool. We also carry a torque wrench. If you have to do a major engine job you can probably buy an inexpensive piston ring expander and valve turning tools on the spot, rather than carrying them around.

Tools for an automatic transmission are too specialized for most of us to carry, but the standard tools you already

Figure 26. Inexpensive, papery Tyvek jump suits are disposable, yet zip on in seconds if you have to do an emergency repair in your Sunday best. The disposables are found in paint and hardware stores.

have can be used to change the oil and adjust the bands. Check, though, to see if you need special wrenches for the oil plugs if yours is a manual transmission.

The basic tools already listed will change your universal joints but greasing universals calls for a special, non-high-pressure grease gun. Don't let anyone grease yours with a gas station-type pressure gun or they'll blow out the seals. If you have only a few grease fittings, carry a small grease gun. Our coach has 20 fittings, so it's worth it for us to carry a larger, proper-pressure gun.

Wheels and Tires. Probably tire changing equipment came with your coach but if the coach is over, say, 2.5 tons, throw away the screw jack that came with it and invest in a good quality hydraulic jack. It weighs more, but is worth every carat. Try to remove a lug nut with the wrench that came with your coach. If it bends, throw that overboard too and buy a heavy duty, commercial grade, X-style lug wrench. If you're going to overhaul your own brakes, you don't need anything besides what we've already listed, but a C-clamp is handy for pushing pistons back in while you fit new linings. For drum-type brakes it's nice to have the special spring remover-installer sold at auto parts stores.

Spares are Important Too

Just as important as tools to work with are spare parts and supplies that allow you to get rolling again. Many of the same problems and payoffs apply to spares as to tools: they are heavy, they take up lots of space, and it's impossible to cover every possible need no matter how many spares you have. We all have to make painful decisions about what to take and what to abandon. Still there are some spares that you should have aboard, even if you can't install them yourself, because it's unlikely that you'll be able to buy them when you need them.

First item on the list is fan belts. We once drove a friend all over town, stopping at least five places before he found a fan belt to fit one of the most common cars in the country. The more oddball your RV and its equipment, the harder (and more expensive) it becomes to find a fan belt when you need one. One fulltimer broke a belt while on a Flordia freeway. It cost $75 for a tow to the nearest garage, a sleepless night in a noisy gas stop, twice the normal price of the fan belt because he bought it on the freeway, and a high price for a mechanic to install it. If he'd checked the belt for fraying or breaks routinely, and had a spare on hand, he probably could have had a buddy help him change it in the campground for nothing.

Some spares are difficult or impossible to find on the road. Other items are worth carrying because they can be bought cheaply in quantity or in discount stores but cost far more if you have to buy them in desperation at gas stations or campground stores. Still other items are used up as you go, so you need spares on hand.

Here are some of the items to consider carrying:

Engine. If any of these items fail on the road, you're sidelined until they can be replaced, so spares should be carried with you even if everything is new now. Carry an extra fan belt for every size used in your RV, and know for sure the size is right. (If you had a non-standard alternator installed, for example, you may not use the size belt called for in your driver's manual.) Look at the belt itself, which should be marked with the manufacturer's code and the size in either inches or metrics. If it isn't, put a tape measure around the installed belt and note size in inches. In any case, know that your spares will fit.

Take spare radiator hoses, especially if yours are an odd, molded design. They'll keep a long time if you just keep them clean and dark, so the investment you make in spares now will pay off tomorrow. A few extra hose clamps in appropriate sizes come in handy too.

In older vehicles one could use a fuel pump overhaul kit but newer, cheaper fuel pumps can't be repaired. So carry a spare. We also like to have an extra fuel filter element or two. If you pick up a bad load of fuel, and clog one filter, you have a second filter to catch the next slug of crud that comes through the line. It's not the best practice to mix types and brands of oil in your engine, so carry at least enough of your brand to do routine topping-up. If you can carry enough oil for the next oil change, so much the better. If you stick with the most common international brands, such as Quaker State or Shell, you'll be able to be consistent. If you'll be doing oil changes yourself, pick up a spare oil filter when you see them on sale.

Have at least one spare spark plug. They can fail or break. If yours is a diesel, a spare injector is always nice to have aboard. One other spare to consider is a universal joint, since you're stranded without one and can change yours fairly easily. With any of these spares, you'll be able to get back on the road—even if you have to hire someone to install the part—and without paying highway robbery prices.

Chassis and drive. You save greatly by greasing your own RV and the handiest way to carry grease is in a cartridge. Most chassis specs call for a high pressure lithium type lube, which is easily found. Carry a spare tire, and check often to see it is in good repair even if you can't change tires yourself. In hot climates, brake fluid is lost through evaporation. We carry an extra pint so we can routinely fill the reservoir with a known, trusted brand. Our lives depend on the brakes a hundred times a day. We'd rather add transfusions from a clean, sealed can than from the derelict pail of brake fluid that has been kicking around the gas station since heaven-knows-when.

Living quarters. Spares aren't as critical here as they are in your drive train. After all, you can always drive to a motel as long as your coach is driveable. Still, we like to be able to do our own work where and when it's needed. It saves money, time, and the annoyance of having strangers working in our home, cupboards, and closets.

Carry some spare washers if your faucets use them, brass B-nuts for the plumbing (they crack), and an extra sewage valve. If you need a spare, it may be hard to find your size. Light bulbs weigh little, and you save a lot by buying them by the box. Too, the box is the safest way to carry them. We seem to go through clearance lights and reading lights most, and we carry a few spares for all the other sizes too.

Carry spare fuses in every size needed for both your 12V and 110V systems, spare key(s) for your coach somewhere you can get at them in an emergency and, if you have a water filter, a spare cartridge if yours is a hard-to-find size. They are bulky, but don't weigh much.

One of the best things about fulltiming is that feeling of open-road independence. But you're independent only as long as the coach remains mobile. Broken down, you're at the mercy of whatever help is available, good or bad.

Chapter 25
Help for the Fumble-Fingered

"I'm 63, about to retire, and a woman alone," wrote a reader of my Fulltimer's Primer column in Family Motor Coaching magazine. "Fulltiming has been my dream, and I'm about to take off, but I've heard a lot of horror stories about mechanics cheating and over-charging single, older women. Any advice?"

This woman's dilemma doesn't apply only to women, to senior citizens, or to singles. Any time any of us get in over our heads in today's technology, we're fair game. The person who can fix anything electrical may be taken for a ride in a clothing shop. The sharp mechanic may get burned when buying a computer. The plumber may be bamboozled by a TV repairman. The woman who runs a million-dollar aircraft company can be beguiled by a cosmetics sales pitch.

The only defense any of us have against all the charlatans who are waiting for us on the highway, in campgrounds, in service stations, and in every other business we visit, is to know as much as possible about our RV's, how they work, what they need, what harms them, and what sort of service they need when. And that's a tall order.

First, I'll make what may be a Pollyanna observation. Most of our countrymen, I believe, are honest, fair, and hard-working. While there are those service station attendants who sell you oil you don't need, or who will slash one of your tires just to sell you a new one, there are also those who give a break to the elderly, the helpless, the handicapped, or the widow who reminds him of his own mother.

Moreover, the customer is *not* always right. Sometimes he's demanding, cheap, tipsy, unwilling to admit that his own neglect caused something to fail, late for appointments, or thinks he knows more than the mechanic does. Still, I'm an ardent defender of consumer rights, so let's get on to defense strategies.

Begin by studying your owner's manual and all the systems manuals that come with your RV. Know the books backward. They'll tell you how to operate your RV and its equipment, what maintenance and service are needed and when, how to troubleshoot before calling in a professional and, in short, what is expected of you in fulfilling your part of the bargain as an owner-operator.

Talk to others in campgrounds, especially to people who have RV's like yours. Don't take one person's opinion as gospel, but get a concensus from people who have similar vehicles, loads, mileage, and driving habits, about such things as whether you really should need new shock absorbers now that you have 45,000 miles on the RV, how long brake pads should last in your kind of operation, or how others' tires are wearing.

Keep notes, and soon you'll have a good "feel" for how long things should last. Ask too about how things feel or sound or look when they begin to go. Vee belts, hoses, tires, shock absorbers (when they leak oil), and oil seals are among those things which your eyes will tell you are deteriorating. Your ears can tell you when vee belts, tires, mechanical items such as universal joints and wheelbearings, windshield wiper motors, and the exhaust system are changing. Use your nose to tell you about leakage in fuel, oils, or sewage, transmission over-heat, electrical problems, dragging brakes, or propane leaks.

In short, learn to sniff, listen and look for abnormalities. Even experts won't have the ear you do for the sound of your own engine. By keeping attuned to the everyday look, sound, and feel of your own rig, you'll become your own best diagnostician. You may not know that something is wrong and if so, what. But you *will* know that something is different and can have it investigated.

Since mechanical troubles almost never heal themselves, early warnings can clue you that you need preventive maintenance or a repair well before highway breakdown. This in turn allows you to choose your own time, place, and mechanic based on convenience and price comparisons rather than being at the mercy of the handiest service station. By keeping careful records, you'll also know when it's time to do routine maintenance tasks which are required every so-many months or so-many miles.

Unless you're handicapped, don't just hand your credit card out the driver's window and let service station attendants fill your tanks. It's during such times that most horror stories occur: a dishonest person may slit a hose, drop oil under a shock absorber to convince you you need a replacement, or stick an ice pick into a tire. A filler cap could be forgotten, or put on too loosely. A soft tire or a leak could go unnoticed.

Check and fill your own tires, oil, cooling system, batteries, drinking water, and automatic transmission oil. Service your own holding tanks, clean the hoses, and put them away yourself. There's no reason why any driver, no matter how little he or she knows about maintenenace, cannot do these tasks. In doing them you save time, money, and the chance of being cheated. Moreover, you know the job has been done correctly for *your* vehicle. Examples: tires shouldn't be checked while hot; you should be consistent in the brand of motor oil you use; not all automatic transmissions are checked the same way. Even an honest mechanic could unknowingly cause trouble.

Not all mechanics allow you in the shop, nor is it practical for you to watch his every move. Still there are times, such as when propane tanks are being filled, when you can observe that the meter or scale are set properly.

Few outsiders can know as much about your vehicle, your driving habits, your maintenance history, and your needs than you do. Armed with this knowledge, you may be a better mechanic than you realize.

The Walk-Around Checklist

There's one preventive maintenance step which can be understood and accomplished by anyone, no matter how mechanically inept, and it can benefit everyone. Simply walk around the RV before you pull away. Do it every time you start up, no matter whether you've been in the campground a month or stopped at a roadside phone booth for two minutes.

This walk-around can help you spot obstruction in your path, and give tip-offs that something is about to fail, break, fall off, or run out. This in turn allows you to choose the time and place of your maintenance, rather than having to rely on the garage closest to where you break down or on the mechanic at the garage where the tow truck drops you.

Here's how:

This is a routine that is almost a religion with savvy drivers, particularly truckers and other professionals. How many times have you driven away from a campground and suddenly wondered, miles down the road, whether you remembered to lock an access door, bring your power cord or sewer hose, or pack your charcoal grill?

We've found all sorts of things lying at campsites, forgotten by rushed campers. Once we followed a coach for several miles, trying to tell the driver that a hammer was lying forgotten on the back bumper. He ignored us, and probably lost a good tool when he hit the next railroad track. You've seen it yourself: a good garment ruined because it was hanging out of a closed door and dragging on the ground, brand new sewer hoses along the roadside where they had fallen out of an unlocked bumper, loose lashings on a roof rack allowing a tarp to flap in the wind while everything soaked up the rain.

Some losses are even more tragic. Campground saplings are ruined by backing vehicles, dogs killed, children maimed. In addition to the normal start checklist that you go through before each trip, make these a habit:

Each time you stop, look at all the tires to see if any have softened or picked up nails or cuts. You've seen truckers walk around tapping inside and outside duals with a billy club. Adopt the habit because the sound will tell you whether both tires are inflated equally. It's the easiest, cleanest, most reliable way to check hot tires. (Use your pressure gauge only on cold tires, and when compressed air is available.)

Glance around the coach for any leaks. A puddle of fuel, oil, or water after you've parked for a while could be your clue that trouble is brewing. Learn to tell the difference between normal air conditioner condensate and a cooling system leak.

At night, snap on all the lights and walk once around to see if they're all working. Have someone check the back-up and brake lights for you once in a while.

If you've taken anything out of the coach, or brought anything to the coach, think through whether everything is aboard. Did you leave your wallet or address book in the phone booth? A bag of potatoes in the bottom of the grocery cart? Your hose on the gas station's water faucet? Your lug wrench in the grass? Your sweater in the restaurant?

Are there any notes you should make about this stop, such as mileage, a name of a garage or new friend, an address of a restaurant, a telephone number? If you do find you've been cheated later, you'll have the name of the mechanic and the address of the station. If you've left anything behind, you'll have the phone number of the campground.

Look up, to make sure you've closed the windows you want closed when you're driving. Check the roof rack, tie-downs, covers, bike racks, hitches. Check every accessory door to make sure it's securely fastened and the fuel cap to make sure it's screwed on tight. If you're towing a car, check it as well.

Is the way clear ahead? Behind? Overhead? Beneath? Pay special attention to curb drop-offs, choosing your route so your overhang won't scrape on the slope, and to any overhead portico's or canopies which are too low for your height (which you should know in exact feet and inches).

Use the time not just looking for trouble spots, but to gear yourself up for the responsibility of taking the wheel and giving all your attention to the road. Some drivers use this time for a short prayer or meditation. In any case, knowing that you've checked everything ahead of time, you can now relax and concentrate on the hazards of the road.

Chapter 26
Safety and Security

We can all drive away from a job, from unpopular neighbors, from city noise, and from metropolitan air pollution, but none of us can escape crime or road hazards. Here are some tips on dealing with both.

Personal Safety

At this writing, not all states yet have seat belt laws, but the trend is towards requiring belts. Australia and New Zealand have tough seat belt laws which place the burden on the driver to see that passengers are protected. The countries have had to close some rehabilitation facilities in some hospitals, because so many fewer people have been maimed. In Europe, insurance companies refuse to pay claims from those who are injured while not using seat belts.

Let's deal with some of popular myths that continue to keep people from using this simple lifesaver.

Myth: "I don't want to be strapped in. The vehicle might burn. Besides, I'm better off if I'm thrown free."

Truth: If you stay with the car, you are 25 times less likely to be hurt than if you're thrown out. We all have heard of cases where people survived by being thrown clear, but for every one of them there have been two dozen people who were killed or maimed either by hitting the ground on being thrown out, or because they were hit by an oncoming car.

Hundreds of injuries occur each year in non-crash incidents when people simply fall out of vehicles. In Florida recently, a 17-year-old mother was charged under the state's child restraint law because her baby fell out when an unlatched door swung open. The baby landed on the highway, and was run over by a following car.

Fire occurs in only one crash in ten. If the vehicle does burn, you have a better chance of freeing yourself and getting out if you were strapped in because you are less likely to have been knocked senseless. Even in fairly mild crashes, victims have burned to death because they were unconscious. The same is true for vehicles that go into the water. The less you are injured on impact, the better able you'll be to find a way out of a submerged vehicle. In Holland, where vehicles can so easily go into canals, courses in underwater escape are given. In them, seat belt use is emphasized.

Myth: "I'm the driver. Seatbelts are OK for the kids in the back, but I have the wheel."

Truth: As the driver you have a greater responsibility to use your seat belt. Even a mild impact from the side could knock you out of your seat and away from the wheel, preventing you from recovering after a swerve. The passengers who depend on you for their survival are deprived of whatever control you might have used to bring the vehicle to a safe stop. Drivers who are thrown against the steering column and then into the windshield can sustain the most severe injuries of all.

Myth: "I can hang on if I see a crash coming."

Truth: It's physically impossible to support your weight in anything but a hard stop. The fiercest carnival rides exert no more than about 1.5 G's, and it's unlikely you were able to move when hanging upside down or when pasted against the side of a whirling ride. Yet occupants in crashes as slow as 5 mph, depending on the crumple rate of the vehicle and other factors, can pull up to 20 G's. If you weigh 100 pounds, you'd have to support 2000 pounds just to keep your body in place— and that assumes that you saw the crash coming in the first place.

Myth: "My cousin (husband/ barber's wife/ best friend) is an emergency room nurse and says seat belts cause lots of injuries."

Truth: Nurses see only survivors. Many of those who use no seat belts go straight to the morgue. Although only about 15% of the general public use seat belts, 73% of the faculty members of Harvard Medical School use them. Even pregnant women are better off when wearing seat belts in an accident.

Myth: "Seat belts are uncomfortable".

Truth: So is a body cast, wheelchair, neck brace, or a white cane.

Myth: "I can't get my passengers to buckle up".

Truth: You have state law on your side in many instances. If not, urge your crew to use belts anyway. We have found that the *real* reason many people don't buckle up is (1) they are self-conscious about their weight and are embarrassed at having to re-adjust the belt, (2) they are afraid you'll be insulted if they buckle up because it looks like they don't trust your driving or (3) they just plain forgot.

In only one case have we met a person who wouldn't use a belt because of a traumatic personal experience. He'd been first on the scene of a burning wreck and been unable to get the victims free from their seat belts. That was, however, in the days before metal-to-metal latches made seat belts easy to release. Tragic as this case was, the numbers still favor seat belts.

Myth: "Seat belts are OK on long trips, but I don't bother with mine around town".

Truth: Most highway deaths occur at speeds below 40 mph, and within 25 miles of home.

Myth: "Seat belts are for wimps".

Truth: You mean like airplane pilots and race car drivers? The average seat belt wearer, according to Changing Times magazine, has a college education and is between 25 and 34 years old.

The statistics are undeniable, and more and more businesses are putting their money where their mouth is. State Farm insurance will double our coverage if we are injured in our motorhome while wearing seat belts. For a time General Motors was offering $10,000 to the estate of anyone who was injured fatally while wearing a seat belt in a new GM car.

Fire

In recent years, RV manufacturers have been required to put escape windows or doors into their rigs, but some earlier RV's had only one door. If you have a window escape hatch, make sure you know where it is and how to open it. On many RV's we've seen, quick-release windows were not well marked.

We carry a couple of fire extinguishers, and they are serviced annually. The new Halon extinguishers are a boon to fulltimers because they leave no residue behind. Dry powder, by contrast, is messy and corrosive. If you carry a dry powder extinguisher, drive with it on its side every so often, to shake up the contents. The powder can pack down from vibration and may not give a full charge when you need it.

When you take a dry powder extinguisher for its annual re-charge, ask the serviceman to let you set off the charge. He has a special place where this is done. This hands-on experience will give you practice with what to push, pull and press, will show you how far the charge shoots, and will give you an idea of how long a spurt will last.

Decide how you and your family would get out of the RV in various emergencies: a fire at the stove, a fire in the engine room, an accident where you landed on one side or the other.

Staying Visible

When you must stop at the side of a highway to change a tire or handle some other breakdown emergency, it's important that other drivers see you in plenty of time to slow down,

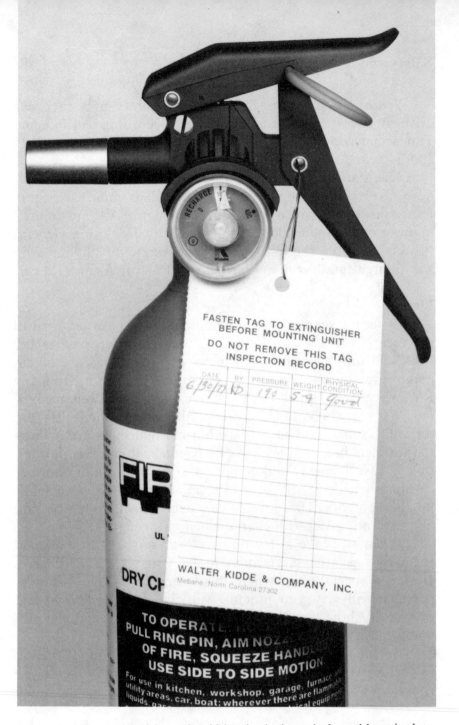

Figure 27. Fire extinguishers should be checked regularly and kept in date.
Photo Credit Walter Kidde.

stop, change lanes, or otherwise avoid you. The brighter the signal you can supply, the safer you'll be. First, get everyone out of the RV and well away from the road. If you have a hand-held CB, one of you might announce on Channel 19 every few minutes that there's an RV changing a tire at Mile Marker so-and-so. Set out whatever lights, flares, or signs you have.

Flares are good, but a strobe light is even better. Ours is called an ACR Firefly, is the size of a pack of cigars, and is so powerful it is used by firemen in smoke-filled buildings. The Firefly is sold in marine supply stores and catalogues.

Guns

The debate over the use of guns for personal protection can be settled in a forum other than this one. If you are anti-gun, there's no more reason to have one in your RV than in any other home. If you believe that having a gun in your home can make you safer, you probably will want one in your RV-home. The National Rifle Association, 1600 Rhode Island Ave. NW, Washington DC 20036 is an excellent source of information and training in safe procedures.

The one difference between keeping a gun in your home and in your RV, is that your RV comes under the laws regarding vehicles, not domiciles. A booklet, *Transporting Personal Firearms* is available for $4.95 from Sparrow Publishing House, P.O. Box 817, Boulder City NV 89005. It lists, state by state, laws regarding gun possession. It's an invaluable guide to staying on the right side of the law (and state laws vary so widely that this will not be easy) as you travel in U.S.A.

Theft

One very simple, cheap step can protect you and your RV. Simply paint a big, bright number, letter, or distinctive sign as large as you can on the roof. If your RV is stolen or you need help in some way from the air, this will help find and identify your camper.

The second security step, again requiring no investment, is to close the curtains when you're not aboard. Passersby can see where you have a television, cameras, radios, or a purse, break a window, grab an item, and make a clean getaway even in crowded parking lots at high noon. In any RV, close and lock windows and doors when you're not home, leaving only overheads open for ventilation. Where possible, mount electronics out of sight and in lockable mounts.

If your RV has no locks on the service doors, buy and install them except on propane access doors, where locks are not permitted. Padlock the spare tire, and buy a lock for the fuel cap. Have good locks for all doors, even if you have to add some.

Other very simple, non-combative steps can be taken. If you have a CB radio in your bed compartment, you can use it to call for help without being seen by thieves who are rifling your tow car. If you have switches for outdoor lights, a microphone for your loud hailer, and/or a siren near your bed, you can activate them and scare thieves into the next county before you even get your pants on.

Once when we were in Fort Lauderdale, we met an RV owner who had left his motorhome in the parking lot of a boat yard while he left town for a week on business. Pranksters had unplugged the camper so, when the owner came back, everything in the refrigerator and freezer was ruined—and the stench when he opened the door was almost audible.

We've had our power cord pulled out in campgrounds, sometimes by accident and other times just by folks who felt they needed the plug more than we did. It's easy to rig a signal light. Simply plug a cheap night light into an outlet. When the power goes off, it goes off. We have a small jewel light wired in near the bed. When the power is on, it makes an unobtrusive glow. When it goes off, we soon notice because we're so accustomed to seeing it.

Alarm Systems

Before ordering a new RV, see what the manufacturer already provides, or can build in as an optional extra. Newell Coach Company, for example, supplies as standard equipment

(1) a smoke detector in the bedroom ceiling, (2) propane sniffer with audible warning and safety shutoff, (3) two Halon fire extinguishers installed inside and one carbon dioxide extinguisher in the engine compartment, (4) high-temperature warning and shutdown for the engine and (5) a burglar alarm installed with a manually operated "panic" switch in the bedroom.

There are dozens of alarm systems available for RV's and boats. (Marine systems are also 12V but are better quality because they're designed to work in a damp, salty atmosphere.) Some of the companies that make them have been around for years, but hundreds more have come and gone so fast that we didn't think it was wise to provide a list in this book.

See what's available on today's market by checking current catalogues such as Sears or Heathkit. A good camping supply store or marine electronics outlet will be able to show you some good alarms. One of the best sources is Radio Shack, with outlets throughout the country.

The most exotic systems have a dozen or more functions. They signal a break-in, window breakage, removal of an item such as a television, or the pressure of someone stepping on your doormat. In addition, the fancy systems sound off if your refrigerator warms up, the toilet leaks, the engine overheats, or you're being monitored on radar.

American Van Equipment, 212 Gates Rd., Little Ferry, NJ 07643 (request their catalogue) offers the Night Hawk which plugs into a cigarette lighter. If someone opens any door or hood which has a light, it senses the voltage draw, and sounds an alarm. It also signals glass breakage, jacking up of your vehicle, movement, or forced entry. For another $40 you can get an external siren. When the siren kicks in, so does a light that flashes the word "Help".

Some alarms shout "Burglar" or "Fire". Others can be hooked up to a remote alarm, so you'll get a signal in your trailer if someone messes with your tow car. Some operate by radio so you'll get a signal through a little pocket device if someone tampers with your RV when you're not aboard.

The most effective systems are those that have both a strong audible signal, and a brightly visible one such as a strobe light mounted on the roof. In a crowded parking lot, many people hear an alarm bell, but may not be able to spot the trouble in time to foil a break-in unless a visible signal catches their attention.

Chapter 27
The End of the Road

Every story has an end, so even if you don't already envision the end of your fulltiming story it's not too soon to give it some thought. For a few fulltimers, the roaming life ends dramatically with death, a divorce, illness, a family crisis. For some others, things just grind down to a sour stop. With these people—and we all meet them—all the magic and motion has gone out of fulltiming but they just don't have enough oomph to do something about it.

For most of us, though, fulltiming comes to an end to be replaced with some new adventure. As long as you and your spouse or family keep communicating and caring about each other, the transition out of fulltiming can be just as exciting as the move into your RV.

One of the best things about fulltiming is that it gives you a lingering look at every part of the country. No longer a vacationer now, the fulltimer can linger long enough to become part of a community, join a church and clubs, make friends, perhaps find a job, look over neighborhoods. Yet,

living in the RV, you can do all this without having to make
so drastic a commitment as setting up a household.

One summer while we were fulltiming, we went to a state
where we thought we wanted to settle down. For months we
made the rounds with real estate agents, looking at property.
We loved the community for its good libraries, symphony,
writers groups. The climate was perfect in summer, warm by
day and cool by night. Then gradually we began to discover
the fly in the ointment. Our bank statement from a local bank
reflected a debit for a state tax we didn't know existed. A
widow friend told us how she was struggling to pay her inheritance tax. When the home is in the names of both husband
and wife, this state makes the surviving spouse pay inheritance
tax on his/her half of the family home!

Then fall came and with it a damp cold. Two cold fronts
later, we had discovered arthritic joints we never knew we had.
Between the taxes and the damp winters, we ruled out settling
here.

Another time we found a beautiful piece of land in the pine
woods area of a southern state. With the owner's permission,
we parked our RV on it for a few nights while we looked it
over. One night, when the wind shifted, we realized the land
was close downwind from a pulp mill that spewed out a sicken-
ing, sulphurous stink. Camping on another piece of land we
were close to buying, we realized that it was on a flood plain.
What now was a lovely trout stream would become a raging
torrent in spring.

In another state we liked, we realized that the 6% sales tax
was collected on everything including food. We decided that
our food bills were bad enough without settling in a state where
another $6 per $100 would be added to our food budget.

Along the Florida coast we found some pretty, wooded
acreage but we knew the state was deep in a drought cycle.
Living in our motorcoach, we stayed in the area, getting
acquainted. Then, after the next really good downpour, we
visited the acreage again. It was deep in mire. People on
neighboring land told us they had constant septic tank prob-

lems because the land was so low. Since then, normal rain patterns have returned to that area, and the people who bought land there during the drought years are living in a near-swamp.

In some areas, living in our coach, we have discovered that well water tastes bad or stains clothes. In others that population growth was so out of control that roads, sewers and other services were falling behind. In others that summers were too steamy or floods too likely. In one mountainous area we learned that much of the prettiest, highest land couldn't qualify for septic tanks because the land was solid rock with little soil. Along some stretches of the coast, we found sand flies unbearable.

No state and no climate is perfect, but when you're full-timing you can experience all climates, all seasons, all wind directions, many different neighborhoods, before you buy or build a home and settle down. You can live among the people who will be your neighbors, read the local papers, sit in on local council meetings, learn about—or even pay— local and state taxes and license fees. And all the while you're investigating, you're living comfortably in your own, rolling home ready to move along the minute you don't like the set-up.

When we first went fulltiming, it was a step taken over many months, with lots of praying and planning. It's the same when you decide to leave fulltiming to buy a house, enter a retirement community, resume a career, or start a family. If you wait until you're too fed up, too broke, too cold, too hot, or on the verge of divorce, it's too late to act with restraint, economy, and prudence.

For us, changing from fulltimers to part-timers again was a happy, positive time. We bought some land in an area we liked, camped on it from time to time when we happened to be in the area, and kept on truckin'. In time, we decided to have a house built but we locked the doors and hit the road as soon as it was finished.

It wasn't a time of discontent or rush but a time when one lifestyle was turning into another. Part-timers again now, we have rediscovered the fun of living in a house, having a workshop and space galore, gardening. Yet we know that we have the energy, the know-how, and the right RV to return to fulltiming any time we care to. Moving aboard should be a running to, not an escape from. Moving out of your coach, to become RV vacationers again, can be the same thing.

Fulltiming allows you to travel anywhere, on any schedule you please. It is an endless summer and, for some, an endless road. For others of us, however, fulltiming is just another adventure to be replaced someday by new adventures. As long as the step is made with all the same unhurried care, precaution, and mutual consideration that got you into fulltiming in the first place, moving on by moving off is just one more of the pleasures of being an RV traveler in the first place.

Appendix I

Fill out these pages, but not until after you have read the entire book. More information on the costs of postage, insurances, cellular phones, and other items is contained in several chapters. The closer you are to departing, the more attuned these figures will be to today's cost of living.

If you like, make several photo copies of these pages. Fill out one set before you take off and another set after your first year of fulltiming. Each year you'll be able to refine and re-tune your budget as you get to know your own needs, and those of your RV better and better. See chapter 8 for a discussion on costs.

Fulltiming Income:

Business income   _____

Estimated Interest   _____

Expected return on investments   _____

Pension   _____

Rental income   _____

Social Security   _____

Other   _____

      Fulltiming Total Income   _____

Continuing Expenses:

List here expenses from your present life which will continue when you go fulltiming:

Admissions   _____

Alimony, child support   _____

Annuities   _____

Clothing, linens   _____

Dry cleaning   _____

Dues   _____

Gifts, charity   _____

Food, beverages   _____

Insurance, health   _____

Insurance, life   _____

Medical, dental   _____

Mortgage, home maintenance   _____

Retirement Plan   _____

Time payments   _____

Other: _____

      Total Continuing Expenses   _____

Future costs, known
    List here those expenses you can learn by doing some homework.
Cellular phone service   _____
Insurance, RV   _____
Insurance, other   _____
Licenses (RV, tow car, drivers)   _____
Mail forwarding   _____
Management services
  (house, business)   _____
Payments, RV   _____
Payments, other   _____
Propane   _____
Schooling   _____
Storage, household goods   _____
Other   _____
        Total Future Costs, Known   _____

Future costs, educated guess (see text)
Batteries, per 2-4 years   _____
Campsites   _____
Coin laundry   _____
Fuel   _____
Generator fuel, car   _____
Hobbies (photo lab, green fees)   _____
Maps and guidebooks   _____
Oil   _____
Postage   _____
Taxes, federal   _____
Taxes, state   _____
Telephone, long distance   _____
Tires, per 50,000 miles   _____
Tolls   _____
Transportation (tow car, bikes,
  taxi, rental car)   _____
Other   _____
        Total Future Costs (ed. guess)   _____

Future costs, unkown
  Reserve, transportation (fly home to family or business emergency)
Reserve, family needs   _____
Reserve, uninsured sickness
 or damage   _____
Reserve, repairs   _____
Reserve, replacements   _____
Other   _____
  Total Future Costs Unkown   _____

Appendix II
Useful Names and Addresses

Brand Name Camping Clubs

Airstream Caravan Club, 306 Jackson St., Jackson Center OH 45334

Avion Travelcade Club, 1300 E. Empire Ave., Benton Harbor MI 49022

Barth Ranger Club, S.R. 15, Milford IN 46542

Beaver Ambassador Club, P.O. Box 633, Lebanon OR 97355

Champion Fleet Owners Assn., 5573 E. North St., Dryden MI 48428

El Dorado Caravan, c/o Greg Stewart, P.O. Box 266, Minneapolis KS 67467

Elkhart Travelers RV Club, c/o Agnes Anderson, 2211 W. Wilden, Goshen IN 46526

Fan Trailer Club, c/o Watson P. Pringle, Rt. 7, Hillcrest Dr., New Castle PA 16102

Fireball Caravaner, c/o Joseph Kurmann, 12087 Lopez Canyon Rd., San Fernando CA 91342

Foretravel Motorcade Club, c/o Carla Vinson, 1221 N.W. Stallings Dr., Nocagdoches TX 75961

Globestar Trailer Club, 2026 Burlison, Urbana IL 61801

Holiday Rambler RV Club, 400 Indiana Ave., Wakarusa IN 46573

International Coachmen Club, c/o George Jordan, P.O. Box 30, Middlebury IN 46540

International Skamper Camper Club, c/o Toni Decker, P.O. Box 338, Bristol IN 46507

Jayco Jafari, P.O. Box 460, Middlebury IN 46540

Lazy Daze Caravan Club, 4303 E. Mission Blvd., Pomona CA 91766

Midas RV Travel Club, P.O. Box 991, Mishawaka IN 46544

Serro Scotty Club, c/o Joseph Pirschl, Arona Rd., Irwin PA 15642

Silver Streak Trailer Club, c/o Ray Haas, 7661 Canton Dr., Lemon Grove CA 92045

Starcraft Campers, P.O. Box 913, Mishawaka IN 46544

Winnebago (also Itasca) Travelers Club, P.O. Box 268,
     Forest City IA 50436
Yellowstone National Travelers, P.O. Box 951, Mishawaka
     IN 46544
Campgrounds
** ACI Parks, 12301 N.E. 10th Place, Bellevue WA 98009
* Coast to Coast, 1000 Sixteenth St. N.W., Suite 860, Wash-
     ington DC 20036
* KOA, P.O. Box 30599, Billings MT 59114
** Outdoor Resorts of America Inc., 2400 Crestmoor Rd.,
     Nashville TN 37215
** Thousand Trails, 4800 S. 188th Way, Seattle WA 98188
*&** United Safari, 30 N. 18th Ave., Sturgeon Bay WI 54235
* U.S. Vacation Resorts, 1888 Century Park E. Los Angeles
CA 90067
* Campground chains. Pay by the night, week or month.
** Condominium campsites. Initial investment may be $5000
     or more; rules and benefits vary.
Campground Guides
AAA. Members only
Rand McNally & Company, 8255 N. Central Park Avenue,
     Sokie IL 60076
Trailer Life, 29901 Agoura Rd., 91301
Wheelers Guides, 1521 Jarvis, Elk Grove IL 60007
Woodall's, 500 Hyacincth Place, Highland Park IL 60035
Government Information Agencies
U.S. Army Corps of Engineers, Washington D.C. 20310
National Park Service, Washington D.C. 20240
U.S. Fish & Wildlife Service, P.O. Box 2417, Washington D.C.
     20013
U.S. Forest Service, Department of Interior, Washington D.C.
     20240
National Camping Clubs
     About camping clubs: some are small and local organi-
zations. Others are vast, nationwide networks that offer dis-
counts, group insurance, slick magazines, and other perks.
Some rely on the energies of one or two ramrods, so addresses

change as club officers come and go. Others, such as Good
Sam and the Family Motor Coach Association, have enormous
staffs and a solid business base. The best practice is to write
for information from several of the following:

Canadian Family Camping Federation, P.O. Box 397, Rexdale,
    Ontario

Escapee Club, Box 2870, Estes Park CO 80517

Family Motor Coach Assn., P.O. Box 44144, Cincinnati OH
    45244

Good Sam Club, 29901 Agoura Rd., Agoura CA 91301

Happy Wheelers International, P.O. Box 316, Osceola IN
    46561

International Travel and Trailer Club, 15320 Crenshaw Blvd,
    Gardena CA 90249

Loners on Wheels, P.O. Box 712, Orlando FL 32822

International Family Recreation Assn. P.O. Box 6279,
    Pensacola FL 32522

National Campers & Hikers Association, 1219 Bracy Ave.,
    Greenville MI 48838

North American Family Campers, 3 Long Hill Rd., Concord
    VT 05824

RV Trade Associations

Canadian RV Association, 55 York St., Suite 512, Toronto
    Ont., Canada M5J 1S2

Family Motor Coach Association, 8291 Clough Pike, Cin-
    cinnati OH 45244

**Recreational Vehicle Industry Association, P.O. Box 2999,
    Reston VA 22090** (excellent source of lists of other
    associations including state organizations; also source
    of invaluable consumer publications)

Recreational Vehicle Dealers Association, 3251 Old Lee
    Highway, Fairfax VA 22030 (can supply, for $3.50, list
    of RV rental agencies)

Index